Here I Stand

Here I Stand

AN INSPIRATIONAL TREASURY OF
Martin Luther

COMPILED & WRITTEN BY
STANLEY BARNES

AMBASSADOR

BELFAST, NORTHERN IRELAND
GREENVILLE, SOUTH CAROLINA

Here I Stand
Copyright © 2003 Stanley Barnes

ISBN 1   84030   149 X

Published by the Ambassador Group
Ambassador Publications
a division of
Ambassador Productions Ltd.
Providence House
Ardenlee Street,
Belfast,
BT6 8QJ
Northern Ireland
www.ambassador-productions.com
&
Ambassador Emerald International
427 Wade Hampton Blvd.
Greenville
SC 29609, USA
www.emeraldhouse.com

Contents

❈

❈

Martin Luther

AN APPRECIATION BY DR. J. S. MACINTOSH

D r. John S. MacIntosh was born in Philadelphia on 30th September, 1839. He came to live in Ireland with his widowed mother and they settled in Ballymoney where they had relatives. He studied at Queen's College, Belfast, and also in Scotland and Germany. He was ordained by the Presbyterian Church on 5th November, 1862 and for five years he was minister of the Connor Church, where in 1859 the great Ulster Awakening also known as the Year of Grace had its beginning. In 1868 he became successor to Dr. Henry Cooke in May Street Presbyterian Church in Belfast and served there for thirteen years. The spirituality of his character may be judged from the following inscription, which he wrote in the album of a friend, 'At times I have thought that the commands of God might be put in two short but solemn sentences: Believe in Jesus with all thine heart; live for Jesus with all thy might. The heart full of faith, the hands full of work – and the soul full of peace. After a visit to attend the Pan Presbyterian Council in Philadelphia in 1880 he received a call on his return, to the Second Presbyterian Church, Philadelphia, which he accepted. During this time he was to play a most prominent role in American Presbyterianism, receiving a D.D. degree from Princeton University and in 1905 becoming Principal of the Theological College at San Anselmo, California. It was while ministering to the congregation of Second Presbyterian Church that he delivered this, his famous lecture on Martin Luther.

THERE ARE men who belong to a year, to a decade, to a period; there are men who belong to the ages and live for all time; there are men, fresh and forceful, who belong to a city, to a country, to a continent, and men who belong to the world; there are men who belong to a class, to a particular circle, to a single definite movement, to a special field of distinct struggle, and men who belong to the wide realm of our common humanity, to the round globe of varying interests, manifold thought and universal activity; there are men of whom you say, "they were," and men of whom all competent witnesses declare, "they are" – are today central men, chieftains, summations of the past, explanations of the present, inspirations for the future, fresh forces still and unspent, lights increasing while thousands wax old and are ready to vanish away. And these men to be wondered at; these men "most men, who work best for men;" these men, "to whom nothing of humanity is alien," are the strong, true men to gather round, to study and to learn from.

Art, literature, science, politics, have in their Angelos, Miltons, Newtons and Hampdens their universal, immortal, many-sided chiefs; and shall the Church, revealer of the perfect beauty, guardian and mother of highest song and sublimest prose, friend of the truth and teacher of the perfect law, not have her imperial spirits? Yes, verily; all down her line she has furnished these kinglike children of the King of kings; and curious enough it is, they ever meet us by threes, these mightiest of God's host, overtopping all the remaining host of the covenant-heroes – Moses, Samuel, Elijah; Peter, John and Paul; Athanasius, Augustine and Chrysostom; Patrick, Columba and Boniface; Luther, Calvin and Knox; and of these three, mightiest and midmost, stands manly, merry, massive, masterly Martin Luther, monk of Erfurt and man of the great Emancipation – "A great brother man," "sovereign of this greatest revolution," prophet idol-breaker," "bringer back of men to reality," "true son of nature and fact, for whom these centuries and many yet to come will be thankful to heaven."

This man, whom grace made humble and God made great, belongs to the world's centuries, to the common activities, the broadening thought, the dominant forces and the farthest-reaching influences of to-day and tomorrow. He belongs to the Church universal; his life and labours are telling mightily within the Romish pale as well as without. The Council of Trent and the Westminster Assembly, the wily Jesuit and William Carey, are all linked, though by very different bands, to the monk of Erfurt, scholar, singer, sage, statesman, saint; a joy to real men, triumph and trophy of God's Son and Spirit. "We glorify God in him."

Yes, God we glorify while we recall the man; for this service is no secret canonisation, no subtle hero-worship, no exquisite Protestant idolatry, no unconscious act of most refined deification. We see the sinner who had his hard fight to wage through life with his fallen nature and was saved only by grace, while we thankfully honour the great revolutionary and grand reformer in whom God's grace found a fit instrument and wrought so efficaciously and abundantly for our emancipation.

If Stephen in his masterly apology and Paul in his thrilling roll-call of God's heroes set before their auditors the God crowned victors in the noble fight, why should we not look long and lovingly on those leaders of the sacramental host who have been made more than conquerors through the Christ who loves them and whom they so loved? God's historic word reveals oftenest embodied grace. There we see grace triumphant, and glorify God, who, by his grace, made the men "of like passions" live to be "the praise of the glory of his grace." God's hand and his grace are manifest in the earnest boy of Eisenach, the ardent student of Erfurt, the God-fearing reformer of Wittenburg, and the popular preacher of northern Germany.

THE EARNEST BOY OF EISENACH

It is a sweet, bright September afternoon. I am pushing my way up George Street in this hill-crowned, pine-shadowed, mead-girdled little town on the Horsel, Eisenach, beneath the Wartburg; and as I pause before the little door of a quaint old house, summer sunshine and today's business fade away, and winter cold, and olden industries, and unfamiliar phrases, and curious garb, and strange, pathetic singing, and nightfall, are about. A band of boys, some twelve, some fifteen, one seventeen years of age, are singing, poor scholars, for their bread; and he of seventeen has the broadest brow and deepest eyes and sweetest voice and thinnest cheeks, yes and that evening, saddest face, of any. The door opens and a woman's soft, tender hand lifts the boy's face; a woman's eyes look deep down into those pool-like eyes; a woman's heart pities the thin cheeks; a woman's motherly love goes out to the starving lad whose voice in the village choir had often lifted her nearer to God, and now made her God's helper in the Reformation. "Who art thou, and whose son?" "I am little Martin, and the son of Hans and Marguerethe Luther of Mansfield;" and Dame Ursula Cotta took him from that hour to her home and heart. That day in Eisenach God had "a missing hand," to use Mrs. Browning's striking phrase; and that good woman, like Miriam, said, "Let others miss me; never miss me God;" and wheresoever the Gospel of free grace is preached, let the name of her "content with duty" be told in gratitude and with honour.

It was the grace of God meeting the starving scholar. He is the child of hard wrought parents, the child of prayer, the first born of a pious though somewhat stern home. Near the very centre of Germany – significant fact – in Saxony, is Eisleben, where about midnight of the 10th of November, 1483, is heard the first cry of a new born child, and where, over a newly-swaddled babe, a hard working miner soon bows in earnest prayer, dedicating his boy to God. God accepts the offering and seals the infant Martin Luther to sublime and successful work. Watched by that strong brained, free-souled, keen-witted, industrious and God fearing father, who often knelt by the child's cot wrestling in prayer that rich blessings might be showered on his firstborn; carefully tended and wisely taught by his devoted and wise mother; surrounded by the profitably talking miners, companions of his father; hearkening to the mind stirring tales of travellers who came for trade from other shores; having his strong memory stored with pithy proverbs and suggestive folk lore yet to be frequently and forcibly employed in keen fight and pointed preaching; having his tuneful spirit stirred by songs and hymns born on battle fields or bequeathed by the mine singers – Martin grew for fourteen years in reflective wisdom, and gained in earnest, persevering study all the knowledge Mansfield could yield. In 1497 his father, self sacrificing and lore-loving, resolved to make a well finished scholar of his son.

Accordingly he sent Martin to Magdeburg, and a year afterwards transferred the promising boy, who was already attracting attention by his thirst for knowledge, his strong, independent thinking and sound judgement, to Eisenach, where Wiegand taught and also good Trebonius, who always lifted his hat to the boys of his classes. These masters made him a first rate Latinist and grammarian, as went the times; and Frau Ursula Cotta made him a genial, gently and home loving man, and, better still, an earnest seeker of holiness.

What see I in all these facts of Luther's boyhood? The hand of the Lord. And shall we not glorify him who gave that earnest spirit, that curious mind, that fast gripping memory, that joyous, song-filled heart, that brave, unconquerable spirit to this boy; who made that shrewd father and praying mother train religiously and educate liberally as their means and their day permitted their pious and promising son; who surrounded the lad with a vigourous, self reliant, sober peasantry, making manliness at once easy and necessary; and who raised up friends and teachers wheresoever young Martin went whose lessons and love called forth his large endowments of head and heart and cultivated them rapidly and well? Looking back from those fierce battle hours of Wittenberg and Worms, from the solemn work of the Wartburg and the crises of Augsburg, Nuremberg and Schmalkald, upon these boyish years in Mansfield and Eisenach, I can imaging no better training for Luther's life work; and the hand of the Lord was in that ordering of circumstances – glory be to his name!

THE ARDENT STUDENT OF ERFURT

The scene has changed to the capital of old Thuringia, to the walled fortress on the broad, fat meadows of the Gera, with its splendid Gothic cathedral, the church of Severus and the convent of the Ursulines, to Erfurt of imperishable fame, dearer far to the lovers of truth and gospel light and liberty than the birth places of all the Ceasars; and in this famous Erfurt the most famous and fascinating spot is this orphan asylum, for here is the Augustinian monastery; and in the thought stirring old pile, most thrilling to me, on July 17, 1869, was a little cell, then visible, with a table, bedstead

and chair, for it was the cell which Luther entered upon the 17th of
July, St. Alexis day, 1505, the cell where he and the world were
reborn.

Waiting and thinking in that birth-spot, now alas, swept away by
fire, I felt how quietly God's revolutions arise! Rome in all her
pride is saying, "I sit a queen, and am no widow, and shall see no
sorrow;" her messengers come from England, from Constance, from
Florence, with glad tidings – "The whole earth is at rest and is quiet,"
for the witnesses are dead; and the kings of the earth have given to
the woman, "drunken with the blood of the saints and with the blood
of the martyrs of Jesus, their power and strength."

He that sits in the heavens laughs: he hath chosen to confound
the mighty with a weak thing in this little cell! The excellency of
the power is of God! How still and simple it all is! Yet sublime as
the quietness of God! Yet here was really born "the mighty man
whose light was to flame as the beacon over long centuries and
epochs of the world;…the whole world and its history was waiting
for this man. It is strange, it is great," that out of this quiet cell shall
step forth "a Christian Odin – a right Thor once more with his
thunder hammer to smite asunder ugly enough *Iotuns* and giant
monsters."

As I mused thus with the hero loving Carlyle, the present passed;
the pointer on the dial had gone far backward – well nigh four
centuries – and I am starting back from something awful on the
floor.

Who lies at our feet on the cold damp flags in that death faint?
Who is he to whom the Augustinian brothers are rushing with such
anxious eyes and loving hearts? Who slowly opens sad, searching,
sunken eyes at the sound of the wise brothers' music, that "best
cordial for sorrowful men"? Who holds with death grip that heavy
folio Latin Bible? He is the distinguished student of the most
distinguished university of northern Germany, the eager truth-seeker,
the companion of and chief among the most brilliant scholars of the
university; the Eisenach boy who quickly distinguished himself in
Latin, in philosophy, in patristics and dogmatic theology, in music
and law and oratory, and gained his master's degree with highest
honours after severest tests when he had been only two years at

Erfurt; he is the pious and earnest soul who, finding one day – just when conscience stung most sharply and Sebastian Wimman thundered over him most loudly the terrors of the law – in the university library a Latin Bible, was brought face to face with the question of questions, "How shall a man be just with God?" and who, knowing no better, quicker, surer path to peace than in monastic life, fled to the house of the Augustinian monks, and became their hope and their pride for scholarship, power of speech and sanctity.

That entrance into this Augustinian monastery, with which his independent and clear headed father ever disagreed, was a momentous and perilous course that had started in fear and been maintained through superstition and ignorance; but the hand of the Lord was in it, and so Luther in the clearer light of after days plainly said and thankfully stated.

There of necessity he came into contact with Augustinian theology, preparing Luther to sit at Paul's feet; there he came under the comforting ministry of old Mathesius, who one day, pointing to the clause in the creed, "I believe in the forgiveness of sins," *commanded* him to hope; there he gained fuller light under the sweet instruction of his teacher Arnold; there he was reached by the suggestive thinking of the English Occam, blessed through the influences of Tauler, cheered through the enlightening words of the "German Sermons" and of the Mystics; there, too, he received the hitherto unsupplied, but most needful, instruction in Greek and Hebrew from his friends Johann Lange and Wenceslaus Linz. But in that old monastery, where at the risk of his life he was ardently seeking perfect peace of conscience and the richest stores of knowledge, he won these three things for him and his work the chiefest of all: the friendship of Staupitz, vicar-general of Germany; the calm leisure to study God's word till it lived in his heart and memory; and the peace of God passing all understanding.

Through the favour and patronage of Staupitz, Martin Luther became known to professors at Wittenberg and prelates in northern Germany as the finest theologian and biblical scholar of his time; was made at twenty five years of age professor of philosophy and theology in Wittenberg; was created district vicar for Mussen and

Thuringia, and advanced to the city pastorate of Wittenberg in February, 1517. God's hand is seen in it all: that lonely soul-fight ends in the peace of God; that monastic study made him mighty in the Scripture; his university professorship rounded his scholarship and made him the wonder and the trusted friend of the young students of his day, who afterwards cheered and rallied about him; the support of Staupitz gave him chair and pulpit; and thus when the monk of Erfurt, only twenty five, stripped for his determined fight with Rome, he was a trained athlete and a recognised victor. "Commit thy way unto the Lord; trust only in him, and he shall bring it to pass."

The Lord has ever used weak things to confound the mighty, but never weaklings. Run down the line and see the men of God – Paul and John, Clement and Polycarp, Athanasuis and Augustine, Patrick and Columba, Wycliffe and Huss, Luther and Melancthon, Calvin and Zwingle, Knox and Melville. The Church needs first for her work, saved men, Spirit-born, Christ-loving, Christ like soul-seekers; but, at the same time, the work of the Church and the wants of the world demand, in the second place, that these men should be scholars and students and thinkers, "giving themselves to reading."

Martin Luther, busy among the busiest, gives himself to reading. God gave him the opportunities, the mind, the zeal; and we glorify God in that ardent student of Erfurt, who so mastered his mother tongue that he remade it and fixed its sonorous, flexible speech and facile fullness; who so cultivated Latin and Greek and Hebrew that he made the German Bible speak the loving message of the loving Master; who so practiced the art of simple, idiomatic writing that he filled heart and head at once; who so cultivated popular and robust speech that "his words are half battles," and so gave himself to music that his hymns and chorals ring and thrill like the songs of the redeemed and the chorus of angelic choirs.

God's man is ready for the struggle, and God's moment strikes.

THE GOD-FEARING REFORMER OF WITTENBERG

"The monk Tetzel, sent out carelessly in the way of trade by Leo the Tenth – the elegant pagan pope – who merely wanted to raise a little money," has come to Wittenberg and is selling his indulgences. "Come forward," "forward" – "a soul out of purgatory for a dollar."

Thousands come forward and buy. One man, one lone man, a quiet peaceable recluse, a wasted student, a poor monk, comes forward – not to buy, but to say, "You are a lie; your pardons are no pardons at all, no letters of credit on heaven, but flash-notes of the bank of humbug, and you know it." And that one man, to use again Froude's words, of bravery, honesty and veracity, is the monk of Erfurt.

The afternoon of the 31st October, 1517, the eve of the festival of All Saints, has come, and a little group wonderingly watches an Augustinian monk with the doctor's hood, a man of medium size, whose bones can be counted through his habit, as, standing on the upper door-step of the Castle Church he nails with wasted but firm hand a long sheet of Latin sentences to the door. It is Martin Luther fixing the gauntlet of Christ's truth to Rome's gates and challenging her to battle in the name of the Lord. In that act he takes his place side by side with Peter and John and Paul, with Polycarp and Athanasuis, with Huss in Prague, Savonarola in Florence, and Knox in the court of Scotland and at Edinburgh.

All the issues of that act Martin saw not: we never do see the remotest and greatest results of our acts. One thing he saw, that Tetzel was a devilish seducer, and that the vaunted indulgences, peddled by him under the bull of Leo the Tenth for the completion of Saint Peter's, was a quick path for souls to hell, and that if possible he at least must bar the way. It is the birth-hour of the modern world. How quietly, unpretending, it comes! The fight of emancipation has begun, but begins on a side issue, as all decisive fights open, whether in Church or State.

In fourteen days those quaint-sounding scholastic words have been changed into "smiting idiomatic phrases" for German, French and Italian princes and peasants, into terse English, and soon into every patois of Europe; and the papal world is convulsed. The war of the faith has opened. The spiritual breaker-up of the way is at the head of the host. God's teaching of the man himself is the monk's text in these theses; and it is clearly stated in one of the sentences, "If a man experiences genuine sorrow for sin he receives full remission from penalty and guilt without any letter of indulgence." One other memorable sentence, "Even the pope can remit the guilt of the penitent only so far as the declaration of God's terms of remission."

In those two sentences, the first bringing the personal conscience into direct contact with God and the second defining and so limiting papal and ministerial power, are the beginnings of the Reformation.

Yes, only the beginnings; for though Luther had been to Rome, had been electrified at the Sancta Scala by the Spirit-voice, "The just shall live by faith," and had been horrified by the villainies of the Vatican, and was now blazing with the fires of a holy hatred of Tetzel and his ways, he had to dispute with Tetzel and the Dominicans, with Sylvester Prierias, with Cajetan at Augsburg, with the papal chamberlain Karl von Miltitz at Altenburg, and fiercest, keenest, most momentous contest of all, with Eck at Augsburg, ere he reached the marrow of the gospel, "that a Christian secures forgiveness of endless guilt, reconciliation with God, righteousness before God, peace and salvation by means of a cordial reliance upon the grace of God as revealed in the gospel, and upon the Saviour Jesus Christ."

Now he had reached his theme and his task; and God gave him a mouth and wisdom which papal legates, and time-serving souls like Eck, and selfish cowards like Erasmus, could not gainsay or resist, as well as a heroic might that bore him on to victory. Martin Luther was a many-sided man. You touch in him the many sides of this grand revolution, the manifold and fruitful Reformation. But one thing above all else he did: he placed the lonely Saviour in the midst of dying sinners and said, "Look and live!"

As brave hearted, reunited Germany made, by the sword of her strength, space beside the Rhine for the lonely commanding "Germania" to be the rallying point and inspiration of the Fatherland, so this lion-like hero of the Reformation, by the sword of the Spirit, placed in clear light and in broad space, lonely and commanding, yet attractive, the sweet and sublime form of apostolic Christianity beside the broad, full river of life; and ever since, Christ's one perfect sacrifice, the open way of faith, the waiting, welcoming Saviour, the open heaven, this grace of God justifying all who believe in Christ, have proved the rallying point and the inspiration of the multiplying hosts of the faith of God's elect.

If one thing more than another rises up clear, central, commanding, consoling, in the reformer's field of words and works, it is the Christ of the cross. Stand back; let him be seen today alone – mighty to save to the uttermost all who come. "Behold the Lamb of God who taketh away the sins of the world". Look unto him, sinner, and be saved. Contemplate him, holy brethren, and grow like him. Not church, nor priest, nor ritual; not Bible, nor baptism, nor supper; nothing but Christ, the lonely, almighty Christ, can do helpless sinners good. Oh, solitary, seeking saving Son of God, thou art the Saviour of the sinner, the sanctifier of the saint, the satisfaction of the saved forever! This Christ Luther proclaimed to rich and poor, to the students of the university and the masses of the markets.

THE POPULAR PREACHER OF NORTHERN GERMANY

Away I must turn from such tempting and thrilling themes as Luther's fearless march to Worms and his unquailing daring before the imperial and papal court, from his seemingly hostile arrest and his kindly protective imprisonment in the Wartburg, from his translation of the Bible and his companionship with Melancthon, from his sudden and secret return in 1522 to Wittenberg, from the part played by him during the Peasants' War, from his marriage, June 13, 1525, with Katharine von Bora, from the grand public protest of Spires, April 19, 1526, from the famous Marburg conference and the Augsburg diet, and the thousand activities filling up the great worker's life, to speak of the last grand phase of his reform work, the preaching of the word. All the reformers were the preachers of great sermons, solid with doctrine, full of well-digested thought and close, cogent reasoning. Huss in Prague, Savonarola in Florence, Calvin in Geneva, Knox in Edinburgh and Latimer in London so preached; and Luther in Wittenberg and in Borna, Altenberg, Zwickau, Eulenberg, Weimar, through Saxony and many districts of northern Germany, was no exception. He was indeed a mighty preacher. When he could not in person proclaim the gospel he sent out letters, so that from England to Russia his truth spread and his words stirred or strengthened life.

Every inch a man, an accurate student of philosophy and ethics, an educated lawyer, a telling biblical expositor, a well trained, though not exactly systematic theologian, a close conservative thinker, a skilled rhetorician, a fiery-tongued orator, poetic and pictorial, the common people hear him gladly, and strong-brained men were taxed to the utmost by his profound thinking.

He was a man among men – as one called him, "der erste Bursch der Burschen," the biggest boy of all boys. He loved the children; he knew the plays of youth, the struggles of the market-place, the doubts of the thoughtful, the sorrows of the bereaved, the household feasts and joys and tears, and his country's need, and, Paul-like, he became all things to all men to win them for Christ.

Thus preaching, translating, expounding; thus writing hymns and composing tunes; thus planting schools and fostering colleges; thus fighting the papacy and denouncing despotism; for twenty years more, on went the genial, generous, great-hearted man. Grace marked all his years, and God upheld him through life's battle, nor failed him when, smitten fatally, he lay down to die in the little town where he was born, baptised and consecrated to God.

Half-past two has struck on Thursday morning, the 18th February, 1546; round the dying saint stand his boys, Martin and Paul, with Coleus and Justus Jonas, his loving friend; three times this sinner saved by grace says, "God so loved the world that he gave his only begotten Son;" three times the son going home says, "Father, into thy hand I commend my spirit." – then sleeps, then wakes, then draws one deep, gentle breath, and Christ crowns the conqueror.

What do we as Christian patriots and as churchmen recognise in this Man of the Emancipation? We see, first, the living centre of the long line of light. The witnesses have been often slain, but they have never failed. They stretch from Christ, the faithful and true Witness, down through the thunderous and tumultuous centuries, a line of hallowed heroes, who stand fast and quit them like men. And the great Centre, the living link binding the souls of truth together, is this stalwart Saxon, genial and godly Luther. He was not the only reformer, he was not the first reformer, he was not the reformer who in all gifts surpassed all other; but he was of the yoke-breakers the most truly central, the most largely comprehensive, and the most variously influential. As Paul stood in the apostolate, so to a great degree stood Luther among the apostles of the Reformation. Paul in himself carried the old over into the new, made the true, the essential, the divine of the past dispensation take its place and reappear, grow active and become fertile in the new: Paul was not John, nor Peter, nor James, but he had much of each of the "pillar-apostles": Paul was the most largely human of that unique band. And in Martin Luther I see the resurrection and reappearance of Augustine, of the grand old British missionary, of Aquinas and the philosophical theologians, pioneers of free thought – of Wycliffe and the early and later schools of Oxford reformers, of Huss and Jerome, of Savonarola and the Bohemians: in him I see the man who comprehended in his own large self something of the men of Geneva and of Zurich, of the men of Rotterdam and of Basle, of Edinburgh and of London: in him I see the man who has touched broad, everyday life at most points, and each point touched became a fountain. Like mountain-lake, receiving and guarding the upper waters and supplying the lower streams, Martin Luther saved the waters of the old springs and poured forth a full, fresh flood into the fields of the reformed Church.

Again, we see in this stalwart soldier, shouting out afresh the old battle cries of insulted Wycliffe and murdered Huss, the anointed yoke-breaker who freed his land, and thus other lands, from the intolerable bondage of the papal supremacy. That burning of the papal bull by Luther on the 10th December, 1520, was a world-turning deed. That solemn march of Martin with his fellow doctors, the fire-faced students, and the vast crowds, stirred to their soul-depths and yet silent in awe, down to the Elster gate, out from the city walls, to the river meadows, that prepared pile and that resolute defiant burning by one hot-hearted, fearless, revolutionary monk, amid the cheers of the crowd and beneath the eyes of Europe, was verily all that timid, self-loving Erasmus said - "the beginning of a universal revolution. Now I see no end of it but the turning upside down of the whole world......When I was at Cologne, I made every effort that Luther might have the glory of obedience and the pope of clemency, and some of the sovereigns approved this advice. But lo! and behold, the burning of the decretals, the 'Babylonish captivity;' those propositions of Luther, so much stronger than they need be, have made the evil apparently incurable." Yes, thank God! the "universal revolution" then began, freeing Germans, Swiss, Hollanders and Britons from that dreadful despotism of the Vatican by which kings were deposed at the pleasure of tyrants like Gregory and Leo, or of scoundrels like Alexander Borgia and Balthasar Cossa, whole nations plunged into storm and strife, lands deluged with blood, dragged like the miserable subjects of Henry the Third into foreign wars, cursed with the fell anathemas, and laid under the frightful 'interdict'. Today we have little idea of the terrible thraldom once endured beneath the iron rule of Rome. Hear how the cold-blooded Hume speaks of the interdict: "The execution of the sentence of interdict was calculated to excite the senses in the highest degree, and to operate with irresistible force on the superstitious minds of the people. The nation was of a sudden deprived of all exterior exercise of its religion. The altars were despoiled of their ornament; the crosses, the relics, the images, the statues of the saints, were laid on the ground; and as if the air itself were profaned and might pollute them by its contact, the priests carefully covered them up even from their own approach and veneration. The use of bells entirely ceased....... The dead were not interred in consecrated ground; they were thrown into ditches or buried in common fields, and their obsequies were not attended with prayers or any hallowed ceremony. Marriage was celebrated in the churchyards.......People were debarred from all pleasures and entertainments, and were forbidden even to salute each other, or so much as to shave their beards, and give any decent attention to their person and apparel. Every circumstance carried symptoms of the deepest distress and of the most immediate apprehension of the divine vengeance and indignation." This Roman yoke was broken in the revolution.

We see in this bold revolutionary one of God's chiefest instruments in disenchaining the minds of men. Robertson says: "Luther was raised by Providence to be the author of one of the greatest and most interesting revolutions recorded in history....To rouse mankind when sunk in ignorance or superstition, and to encounter the rage of bigotry armed with power, required the utmost vehemence of zeal, as well as a temper daring to excess." All students know how the German mind has stirred and now stirs the mind of the world. Martin Luther was the mover of these moving minds. After the edict of the Diet of Spires in 1526, Saxony, led by Luther and leading other Protestant states, abolished monasteries and nunneries, released their members to teach and preach, and devoted their revenues to the purposes of education. The effect was immediate and immense. To aid and accelerate the movement came the German sermon, the German Bible and the German hymn. The school and the song were everywhere in the "luther-land," and mind was free. Thus was it likewise in every reformed state. Is it any wonder then that even the humanitarian Frederick von Schlegel should say, "The Reformation was unquestionably a mighty, extraordinary and momentous revolution which has in chiefest part directed the march of modern times, influenced the legislation and policy of European states, and stamped the character of modern science down to our own days"? Luther placed the pope and Rome and the traditions of the elders before the jury of the world's thought: he made his charge, he pleaded his cause, and challenged a verdict, - judge ye! Free inquiry became the right and the duty, yet the necessity, not of the few but of the many, not of the priest but of the people, not of the learned but of all responsible men.

Today it is of the vastest importance to emphasize this fact that knowledge, free thought, advancing science, are the noble children of this holy revolution. The attempt is made to sever free thought and full faith. It is a foolish and foul deed - this robbing of the mother of her children. Even Buckle says, "In the sixteenth century the credulity of man and their ignorance, though still considerable, were rapidly diminishing, and it was found necessary to organise a religion suited to their altered circumstances – *a religion more favourable to free inquiry*.....All this was done by the establishment of Protestantism." And in more sympathetic and eloquent words the great Robert Hall declares, "The Reformation was the great instrument in undermining and demolishing that long-established system of intellectual despotism and degradation. Under the light diffused by the reformers, men awoke from the trance of ignorance and infatuation in which they had slept for ages. They felt those energies of thought and reason which had been so long disused. They began to investigate truth for themselves; they started to that career of genius and science which has ever since been advancing. Had this been the only benefit which it produced, the Protestant Reformation would deserve to be numbered amongst the noblest achievements of mental energy. Viewing it in this light, even infidels have applauded Luther and his associates." Yes, that reformation day was the spark of a glorious revolution: thought was freed from the fetters, the understanding was emancipated, and man became God's "interpreter of nature" once again: and at the centre of that liberation movement were the reformers, with the great Saxon at their head. Thank God for the great yoke-breaker! – he belongs to us all! And we rejoice in him, and honour him as freely and fully as German or Lutheran.

And finally we see in him the anointed champion who gave freedom of conscience, of worship and of home. The monk of Erfurt and student of the old Latin Bible knew the bliss of a free conscience and an open Bible; and he placed the lonely soul in its own awful, personal responsibility face to face with the personal God and the incarnate Saviour, and give them the record of life in simple speech to guide the sinner to peace and the saint to glory. Blessed freedom! The one High priest he showed, and called men to free churches where in their own tongue they heard the wonderful works of God, listened to "all the words of this life" told in their own home-speech, sang the translated psalm and the German chorals or hymns, and worshipped the living God directly and in their own way. Blow the great trumpet! The Lord's jubilee has come. And the home! – oh sweet emancipation! Dear Martin! Lover of childhood, singer for the infants, weeper over the "wee dead;" true-hearted husband, writer of the merry letters home – thou wilt free the home from the yoke of the confession, and save our wives and daughters from that despotism and degradation!

Yes! as we look at the chains snapped asunder, at our deliverance from priest and pope, at our large place of liberty, at the open and full charter of our freedom in this unchained, open Bible; at our free altars, churches and homes, we will remember the Man of the Emancipation, whom God made to stand strong; and we will glorify God in him!

> "Still echo in the hearts of men
> The words that thou hast spoken;
> No forge of hell can weld again
> The fetters thou hast broken."

> "Friend of the slave! and yet the friend of all;
> Lover of peace, yet ever foremost when
> The need of battling freedom called for men
> To plant the banner on the outer wall;
> Gentle and kindly, ever at distress
> Melted to more than woman's tenderness,
> Yet firm and steadfast, at his duty's post
> Fronting the violence of a maddened host,
> Like some gray rock from which the waves are tossed!"

Thus he lived "a true and brave and downright honest man;" and thus he died: - "Reverend father, wilt thou stand by Christ and the doctrine thou hast preached?" – he uttered an audible "Yes!" "Throughout the whole evangelical Church arose a cry of lamentation. Luther was mourned as a prophet of Germany – as an Elijah who had overthrown the worship of idols and set up again the pure word of God. Like Elisha to Elijah, so Melancthon called out to him, 'Alas!' the chariot of Israel and the horsemen thereof!"

He died, yet lives. Luther, the child of the long past, the father of the fertile future – reformer of the reformers, as Spenser and Keats are the poets of poets – the head of the column, with Calvin, his superior in subtle analysis and exact system on the one side, and Knox, his superior in administrative statesmanship and political daring on the other, himself chiefest of the three mighties; with loving Melancthon, dashing Zwingle, farseeing Farel, hesitating Cranmer, dauntless Hamilton and stout Hugh Latimer behind him – thank God for the brave, blunt, bold son of reality – hero of the faith-fight and inspiration of the brave, with spirit independent yet humble, conservative yet radical, critical yet believing and reverent, whose method was search the Scriptures, submit only to Scripture and spread these Scriptures; whose aim was to bring the man and the mind to the light and liberty and life of the gospel. Great man of God, we honour thee and glorify thy Maker!

Great man of the centuries in whom, as Carlyle says, were present "English Puritanism, England and its Parliament, America's vast work these two centuries; French Revolution, Europe and its work everywhere at present," we will honour thee and glorify God in thee, for clearer than the hand of the Caesars, or of Constantine, or of Charlemagne, we see they hand, more commanding thy position, more controlling thy influence!

"True great man – great in intellect, in courage, in affection and integrity, one of our most lovable and precious men! Great, not as a hewn obelisk, but as an Alpine mountain; so simple, honest, spontaneous, not setting up to be great at all, there for quite another purpose than being great. Ah, yes, unsubduable granite, piercing far and wide into the heavens, yet in the clefts of it fountains, green, beautiful valleys with flowers."

"Rest, high-souled Witness! Nothing here
Could be for thee a meet reward;
Thine is a treasure far more dear,
Eye hath not seen it, nor the ear
Of living mortal heard
The joys prepared – the promised bliss above,
The holy presence of Eternal Love.

"Sleep on in peace. The earth has not
A noble name than thine shall be;
The deeds by martial manhood wrought,
The lofty energies of thought,
The fire of poesy,
These have but frail and fading honours: thine
Shall time unto eternity consign.

"And when thrones shall crumble down,
And human pride and grandeur fall,
The herald's line of long renown,
The mitre and the kingly crown,
Perishing glories all!
The pure devotion of thy glowing heart
Shall live in heaven, of which it was a part."

SELECTED SAYINGS OF
Martin Luther

T he impact of a word "fitly spoken" has often been demon-
strated throughout the centuries. Such rich statements of
truth are "like apples of gold in settings of silver" according to
Solomon.

For anyone involved in the art of effective communication, verbal or
written, this collection of quotations from the pen of Luther, many of
which are one liners, encapsulating the wit and ageless wisdom of the
great Reformer, will provide an invaluable reference tool for speakers,
teachers, writers, preachers and students alike.

ABIDING

I had rather be in hell with Christ, than be in heaven without Him.

A dungeon with Christ is a throne, and a throne without Christ is a hell.

I am so busy at this present time I cannot do with less than four hours each day in the presence of God.

ACTION

God loves not the questioner, but the runner.

We are not made righteous by doing righteous deeds; but when we have been made righteous we do righteous deeds.

AFFLICTION

Affliction is the best book in my library.

There is nothing that this passion does not sweeten even death itself.

The fact that Christians are exercised by the cross and by afflictions is a proof that divine grace and benevolence rest on them.

They gave our Master a crown of thorns. Why do we hope for a crown of roses?

I never knew the meaning of God's Word until I came into affliction.

AGE

It would be a good thing if young people were wise and old people were strong, but God has arranged things better.

ANGELS

An angel is a spiritual creature created by God without a body, for the services of Christendom and of the Church.

At death, when we die we have the dear angels for our escort on the way. Those who can grasp the whole world in their hands can surely also keep our souls that they journey safely home.

ASTRONOMY

Astronomy is a beautiful gift of God, as long as she keeps to her own sphere; but if she steps beyond it, and seeks to prophesy future things, as the astrologers do, this is not to be encouraged. I have gone so far in astrology that I believe it to be nothing.

ATONEMENT

Christ took our sins and the sins of the whole world as well as the Father's wrath on his shoulders, and he has drowned them both in Himself so that we are thereby reconciled to God and become completely righteous.

Mystery of mysteries, God forsook God.

BAPTISM

Baptism signifies that the old Adam in us is to be drowned by daily sorrow and repentance, and perish with all sins and evil lusts; and that the new man should daily come forth again and rise, who shall live before God in righteousness and purity forever.

BEAUTY

There is nothing more beautiful in the eyes of God than a soul that loves to hear His Word.

BIBLE

The Bible is alive, it speaks to me; it has feet, it runs after me; it has hands, it lays hold on me.

The Bible was written for a man with a head upon his shoulders.

In this Book thou findest the swaddling clothes and the manger wherein the Christ is laid. Thither the angels directed the shepherds. These swaddling clothes may, indeed, be poor and little; but precious is the treasure, Christ, laid therein.

Let the man who would hear God speak read Holy Scripture.

Scripture is God's testimony concerning Himself.

All the words of God are weighed, counted and measured.

To read Holy Writ without faith in Christ is to walk in darkness.

What the pasture is to the herd, a house to a man, a nest to a bird, a rock to the chamois, a stream to the fish, so the Bible is to the faithful soul.

The Bible is a very large, wide forest, wherein stand many trees of all kinds, from which we can gather many kinds of fruits. For in the Bible we have rich consolation, doctrine, instruction, exhortation, warning, promises, and threatenings. But in all this forest there is not a tree which I have not shaken, and broken off a pair of apples or pears from it. First, I shake the whole apple tree that the ripest might fall, then I climb up the tree and shake each limb, and then each branch, and then each twig, and then I look under each leaf.

My best and Christian counsel is, that all should draw from the spring or well-head; that is, should read the Bible diligently. For he who is well grounded and exercised in the text, will be a good and perfect theologian, since one saying or text from the Bible is worth more than many glosses and commentaries, which are not strong and round, and do not stand the enemy's thrust.

Divinity is nothing but a grammar of the language of the Holy Ghost.

I have made a covenant with God that he sends me neither visions, dreams, nor even angels. I am well satisfied with the gift of the Holy Scriptures, which give me abundant instruction and all that I need to know both for this life and for that which is to come.

I have done nothing; the Word has done and accomplished everything.

Before the Word everyone must give way.

BIBLE STUDY

Scripture is not in our power, not in the ability of our mind. Therefore, in its study we must in no way rely on our own understanding, but we must become humble, and pray that He might bring that understanding to us.

BOOKS

He counselled all, whatever their studies were, to take certain books and read them earnestly; reading one good author again and again, and making themselves so familiar with him that they should be, as it were, transmuted into his flesh and blood.

Through so many commentaries and books the dear Bible is buried, so that people do not look at the text itself. It is far better to see with our own eyes than with other people's eyes. For which reason I could wish that all my own books were buried nine ells deep in the earth, on account of the bad example they may give to others to follow me in writing multitudes of books.

I would like all my books to be destroyed so that only the sacred writings in the Bible would be diligently read.

CAPITAL PUNISHMENT

Government does not belong in the Fifth Commandment.

CHRISTIAN MINISTRY

Let him who wants to counsel others faithfully, first have some experience himself, first carry the cross himself, and lead the way by his example.

CHURCH

God's people and the church are those who rely on nothing else than God's grace and mercy.

Let him who wants a true church cling to the Word by which everything is upheld.

Anyone who is to find Christ must first find the church. How could anyone know where Christ is and what faith in him is unless he knew where his believers are?

The church is not wood and stone, but the company of people who believe in Christ.

Farewell to those who want an entirely pure and purified church. This is plainly wanting no church at all.

COMFORT

Without Christ no one can comfort himself.

CONFESSING CHRIST

If I profess with loudest voice and clearest exposition every portion of the truth of God except precisely that little point which the world and the Devil are at that moment attacking, I am not confessing Christ. 'Where the battle rages, there the loyalty of a soldier is proved.'

CONSCIENCE

My conscience is captive to the Word of God.

You should not believe your conscience and your feelings more than the word which the Lord who receives sinners preaches to you.

CONTENTMENT

Next to faith, this is the highest art: to be content in the calling in which God has placed you. I have not learned it yet.

CONVERSION

To be converted to God means to believe in Christ, to believe that he is our Mediator and that we have eternal life through Him.

CROSS

There is not a word in the Bible which is *extra crucem*, which can be understood without reference to the cross.

DANGER

(There is) no greater danger than no danger at all.

DOCTRINE

Any teaching which does not square with the Scriptures is to be rejected even if it snows miracles every day.

DOUBTING

To doubt is sin and everlasting death.

What will he ever learn who is taught to doubt?

The art of doubting is easy, for it is an ability that is born with us; we derive it from our parents.

DUTY

The right practical divinity is this: believe in Christ, and do your duty.

EARNESTNESS

This is not a time for jest, but for earnest. "Ye are the salt of the earth." Salt bites and pains, but it cleanses and preserves from corruption.

ENVY

Too many Christians envy the sinners their pleasure and the saints their joy, because they don't have either one.

FAITH

Faith, like light, should always be simple, unbending; while love, like warmth, should beam forth on every side, and bend to every necessity of our brethren.

Through faith we do good works. Through good works faith is made visible and comprehensible - as the Godhead cannot be seen nor comprehended; but when Christ became incarnate, He was seen and handled.

The only saving faith is that which casts itself on God for life or death.

Our faith is an astounding thing – astounding that I should believe him to be the Son of God who is suspended on the cross, whom I have never seen, with whom I have never become acquainted.

Faith is the "yes" of the heart, a conviction on which one stakes one's life.

The truth is mightier than eloquence, the Spirit greater than genius, faith more than education.

Faith and human understanding are one against another.

Faith dependeth upon the Word.

Faith is a Christian's treasure.

Faith in Christ destroyeth sin.

Faith maketh us Christ's heritage.

Faith is to build certainly on God's mercy.

Faith taketh hold of Christ, and hath him present, and holdeth him enclosed, as the ring doth the precious stone.

When faith is of the kind that God awakens and creates in the heart, then a man trusts in Christ. He is then so securely founded on Christ, that he can hurl defiance at sin, death, hell, the devil, and all God's enemies. He fears no ill, however hard and cruel it may prove to be.

Right faith is a thing wrought by the Holy Ghost in us, which changeth us, turneth us into a new nature..... Faith is a lively thing, mighty in working, valiant and strong; so that it is impossible that he who is endued therewith should not work always good works without ceasing… for such is his nature.

Faith unites the soul with Christ as a bride is united with her bridegroom.

FAITHFULNESS

Here I stand; I can do no otherwise. God help me. Amen! (His speech at the Diet of Worms)

FALSEHOOD

A lie is like a snowball. The longer it is rolled the larger it is.

Lies are always crooked, like a snake, which is never straight, whether still or moving – never till it is dead – then it hangs out straight enough.

FREEDOM

Christian freedom is no trifle, although it may concern a trifle.

Not only are we the freest of kings, we are also priests forever, which is far more excellent than being kings, for as priests we are worthy to appear before God to pray for others and to teach one another divine things.

If any man doth ascribe aught of salvation, even the very least, to the free will of man, he knoweth nothing of grace, and he hath not learnt Jesus Christ aright.

FREEWILL

In divine and spiritual things we have no free will, but only in name.

If any man doth ascribe aught of salvation, even the very least, to the free will of man, he knoweth nothing of grace, and he hath not learnt Jesus Christ aright.

FRIENDSHIP

To gather with God's people in united adoration of the Father is as necessary to the Christian life as prayer.

GOOD WORKS

The merit of works ceases when righteousness is sought by faith.

Faith, which is given by God's grace to the ungodly, and by which they are justified, is the substance, foundation, fountain, source, chief and firstborn of all spiritual graces, gifts, virtues, merits and works.

Good works are works that flow from faith and from the joy of heart that has come to us because we have forgiveness of sins through Christ.

GOSPEL

God writes the gospel not in the Bible alone, but on trees, and flowers, and clouds and stars.

The law discovers the disease; the gospel gives the remedy.

The law is what we must do; the gospel what God will give.

GRACE

Christ our Lord is an infinite source of all grace, so that if the whole world would draw enough grace and truth from it to make the world all angels, it would not lose one drop; the fountain always runs over, full of grace.

HATRED

Two sins, hatred and pride, deck and trim themselves out as the devil clothed himself in the Godhead. Hatred will be Godlike; pride will be truth. These two are deadly sins: hatred is killing, pride is lying.

HEAVEN

I would not give one moment of Heaven for all the joys and riches of the world, even if it lasted for thousands and thousands of years.

HOLINESS

I am a great enemy to flies; when I have a good book, they flock upon it and parade up and down it, and soil it. It is just the same with the devil. When our hearts are purest, he comes and soils them.

HOLY SPIRIT

The Holy Spirit brings Christ home to us.

Where the Holy Spirit does not preach, there is no church.

The work of the Holy Spirit is going forward perpetually.

Proper understanding of the Scriptures comes only through the Holy Spirit.

HOPE

In our sad condition our only consolation is the expectancy of another life. Here below, all is incomprehensible.

Everything that is done in the world is done by hope. No husbandman would sow a grain of corn if he hoped not it would grow up and become seed.....Or no tradesman would set himself up to work if he did not hope to reap benefit thereby.

HUMAN NATURE

Human nature is like a drunken peasant. Lift him into the saddle on one side, over he topples on the other side.

God uses lust to impel man to marriage, ambition to office, avarice to earning, and fear to faith.

The natural man cannot want God to be God. Rather he wants himself to be God, and God not to be God.

HUMILITY

God creates out of nothing. Therefore until man is nothing, God can make nothing out of him.

IDLENESS

Those who live in idleness are not going in God's but in the devil's ways; they are not living in God's order, for God has ordained work.

IDOLATRY

We easily fall into idolatry, for we are inclined to it by nature; and coming to us by inheritance, it seems pleasant.

That to which your heart clings is your god.

Whatever man loves, that is his god. For he carries it in his heart; he goes about with it night and day; he sleeps and wakes with it, be it what it may – wealth or self, pleasure or renown.

Anything that one imagines of God apart from Christ is only useless thinking and vain idolatry.

INDIVIDUALITY

Every man must do two things alone: he must do his own believing and his own dying.

JESUS CHRIST

In his life Christ is an example, showing us how to live; in his death he is a sacrifice, satisfying for our sins; in his resurrection, a conqueror; in his ascension, a king; in his intercession, a high priest.

JUSTIFICATION

Now the article of justification, which is our sole defence, not only against all the force and craft of man, but also against the gates of hell, is this: that by faith only in Christ, and without works, we are pronounced righteous and saved.

When the article of justification has fallen, everything has fallen. This is the chief article from which all other doctrines have flowed. It alone begets, nourishes, builds, preserves, and defends the church of God. Without it the church of God cannot exist for one hour. It is the master and prince, the lord, the ruler, and the judge over all kinds of doctrines.

I am justified and acceptable to God – even though there are in me sin, unrighteousness, and fear of death.

When by the Spirit of God, I understood these words, "The just shall live by faith," I felt born again like a new man: I entered through the open doors into the very Paradise of God!

Learn to know Christ and him crucified; learn to sing unto him, and say, Lord Jesus, thou art my righteousness, I am thy sin. Thou hast taken upon thee what was mine, and hast set upon me what was thine. Thou hast become what thou wast not, that I might become what I was not.

KINGDOMS

He has rescued us out of the darkness and gloom of Satan's kingdom and brought us into the kingdom of his dear Son.

And if thou be not in the kingdom of Christ, it is certain that thou belongest to the kingdom of Satan, which is this evil world.

LAUGHTER

If you're not allowed to laugh in Heaven, I don't want to go there.

LIVING FOR GOD

I have held many things in my hands, and I have lost them all…..but whatever I have placed in God's hands, that I still possess.

MARRIAGE

Let the wife make the husband glad to come home, and let him make her sorry to see him leave.

Of course, the Christian should love his wife. He is supposed to love his neighbour, and since his wife is his nearest neighbour, she should be his deepest love.

To have peace and love in a marriage is a gift that is next to the knowledge of the gospel.

In domestic affairs I am led by Katie. Otherwise I am led by the Holy Ghost.

Next to God's Word the world has no more precious treasure than holy matrimony. God's best gift is a pious, cheerful, God-fearing, home keeping wife to whom you can trust your goods and body and life.

MIRACLES

The greatest miracle that ever took place on this earth is that the Son of God died the most shameful death on the cross.

MUSIC

Music is a part of us and either ennobles or degrades our behaviour.

The devil does not stay where music is.

I have no use for cranks who despise music, because it is a gift of God. Next to theology, I give to music the highest place and greatest honour.

Music is the best refreshment of a troubled man, whereby his heart is again brought to peace, invigorated and refreshed.

Music is a discipline and mistress of order and good manners; she makes the people milder and gentler, more moral and more reasonable.

OBEDIENCE

I had rather obey than work miracles.

PRAISE

To remember means always to praise.

Only a new man can sing a new song. A person cannot praise God unless he understands that there is nothing in himself worthy of praise, but that all is of God and from God.

You should praise God, not yourself, for all the good you experience or have.

PRAYER

A good prayer must not be too long. Do not draw it out. Prayer ought to be frequent and fervent.

Prayer is the most important thing in my life. If I should neglect prayer for a single day, I should lose a great deal of the fire of faith.

Let us pray and strive; for the word of faith and the prayer of the just are the mightiest weapons.

As a shoemaker makes shoes, and a tailor coats, so should a Christian pray. Prayer is the Christian's business.

Every sigh of a Christian is a prayer: when he sighs he prays.

No man should be alone when he opposes Satan. The church and the ministry of the Word were instituted for this purpose, that hands may be joined together and one may help another. If the prayer of one doesn't help, the prayer of another will.

I have often learned more in one prayer than I have been able to glean from much reading and reflection.

Grant that I may not pray alone with the mouth; help me that I may pray from the depths of my heart.

I have so much to do that I spend several hours in prayer before I am able to do it.

None can believe how powerful prayer is, and what it is able to effect, but those who have learned by experience.

No one prays for anything who has not been deeply alarmed.

Pray and let God worry.

The fewer the words, the better the prayer.

Where there is not faith and confidence in prayer, the prayer is dead.

To be a Christian without prayer is no more possible than to be alive without breathing.

The Lord's Prayer is the prayer above all prayers. It is a prayer which the most high Master taught us, wherein are comprehended all spiritual and temporal blessings, and the strongest comforts in all trials, temptations and troubles, even in the hour of death.

Before praying give thanks and before teaching pray.

The intellect makes the prayer, but the feeling makes the cry.

Believing in God means getting down on your knees.

PREACHERS

It is commonly said that these are the three qualifications which mark a good preacher: First, that he step up; secondly, that he speak up and say something (worthwhile); thirdly, that he knows when to stop.

God certainly has not instituted the office of the ministry in order to produce secure and lazy preachers for Himself.

PREACHING

Preaching is truth through personality.

When I preach I regard neither doctors nor magistrates, of whom I have above forty in my congregation; I have all my eyes on the servant maids and on the children. And if the learned men are not well pleased with what they hear, well, the door is open.

I am certain that when I enter the pulpit or stand at the lectern to read, it is not my word, but my tongue is the pen of a ready writer.

He that has but one word of God before him, and out of that word cannot make a sermon, can never be a preacher.

The highest worship of God is the preaching of the Word; because thereby are praised and celebrated the name and the benefits of Christ.

To have prayed well is to have studied well.

Prayer, meditation and temptation make a minister.

It is not necessary for a preacher to express all his thoughts in one sermon. A preacher should have three principles: first, to make a good beginning, and not spend time with many words before coming to the second point; secondly, to say that which belongs to the subject in chief, and avoid strange and foreign thoughts; thirdly, to stop at the proper time.

PREDESTINATION

All objections to predestination precede from the wisdom of the flesh.

In the wounds of Christ alone is predestination found and understood.

PRIDE

If you feel or imagine that you are right and suppose that your book, teaching or writing is a great achievement....then, my dear man, feel your ears. If you are doing so properly, you will find that you have a splendid pair of big, long shaggy asses' ears.

PROSPERITY

Ah, what a calamity it is that man degenerates more in prosperity than in adversity.

PROVIDENCE

Our Lord God likes to act otherwise than we suggest.

REASON

Christ alone is the Light and the Life of all men, not our reason.

RELICS

What lies there are about relics. One claims to have a feather from the wing of the angel Gabriel, and the Bishop of Mainz has a flame from Moses' burning bush. And how does it happen that eighteen apostles are buried in Germany when Christ had only twelve.

REPENTANCE

To do so no more is the truest repentance.

A penitent heart is a rare thing and a great grace; one cannot produce it by thinking about sin and hell. Only the Holy Spirit can impart it.

RESURRECTION

Our Lord has written the promise of the resurrection, not in books alone, but in every leaf in springtime.

This corrupt and feeble body cannot continue as it is. Therefore it is best that the Potter should take the vessel, break it in pieces, make it mere clay again, and then make it altogether new.

RICHES

Riches are the least things on the earth, and the least worthy gift which God can give a man. What are they to God's Word? yea, to bodily gifts, such as beauty and health; or to the gifts of the mind, such as understanding, skill, wisdom? Yet men toil for them day and night, and take no rest.

RIGHTEOUSNESS

Ah, how large a part of righteousness it is to want to be righteous.

True righteousness has compassion; false righteousness has indignation.

SATAN

The devil, that lost spirit, cannot endure sacred songs of joy. Our passions and impatiences, our complainings and our cryings, our alas! and our woe is me! please him well; but our songs and psalms vex him and grieve him sorely.

The devil has not indeed, a doctor's degree, but he is highly educated and well experienced, and has moreover, been practising, trying, and exercising his art and craft, now well-nigh six thousand years. No one avails against him but Christ alone.

The devil has a great advantage against us, inasmuch as he has a strong bastion and bulwark against us in our own flesh and blood.

Faith understands that the devil has been conquered, death killed, and heaven opened; but reason does not know it.

SCRIPTURE

None understand the Scriptures save those who prove them through the cross.

Every prophet should be interpreted as speaking of Jesus Christ.

SECOND COMING

There are three distinct comings of Christ designed that the day of his coming should be hid from us, that being in suspense, we might be as it were upon the watch.

If Christ were coming again tomorrow, I would plant a tree today.

SICKNESS

A doctor is our Lord God's repairman of the human body, just as we theologians are repairmen of the soul to remedy the damage the devil has done.

SIN

I have no other name than sinner; sinner is my name, sinner is my surname.

The recognition of sin is the beginning of salvation.

Of the enormity of sin no man was ever convinced but by the Holy Spirit Himself.

We sin and err without ceasing.

Nothing is easier than sinning.

SINFUL NATURE

I more fear what is within me than what comes from without.

SUBMISSION

A Christian man is the most free lord of all, and subject to none; a Christian man is the most dutiful servant of all, and subject to everyone.

SUFFERING

Our suffering is not worthy the name of suffering. When I consider my crosses, tribulations, and temptations, I shame myself almost to death, thinking what are they in comparison of the sufferings of my blessed Saviour Christ Jesus.

In Christ sufferings are salutary..... Faith causes sufferings to be useful and injuries to be pleasant.

TEACHERS

A pastor and schoolteacher plant and raise young trees and saplings in the garden. Oh, they have a precious office and work and are the finest jewels of the church; they preserve the church.

No calling pleases me as well as that of schoolmaster; nor would I more gladly accept any other calling.

It takes persons of exceptional ability to teach and train children aright.

TEMPTATION

The essence of temptation is that we forget the present and covet the future, like Eve in Paradise.

Temptation makes us live in the fear of God, walk circumspectly, pray without ceasing, grow in grace and in the knowledge of Christ, and learn to understand the power of the Word.

My temptations have been my masters in divinity.

One Christian who has been tempted is worth a thousand who haven't.

The greatest temptation of all is to have no temptation.

Do not argue with the devil and his temptations and accusations and arguments, nor, by the example of Christ refute them. Just keep silent altogether; turn away and hold him in contempt.

Every age, even among the godly, has its peculiar temptations. Lust is especially tempting to the age of youth; ambition and vainglory, to the age of mature manhood; avarice to old age.

Christ, who was tempted in our flesh, is the best Intercessor before God in all temptations.

THANKSGIVING

Christ was offered once for all; now He requires nothing but that we should give Him thanks for ever.

Thanksgiving makes our prayer bold and strong, easy, moreover, pleasant and sweet; feeds and enkindles them as with coals of fire.

TRUST

Where our trust is, there is our God; where the treasure, there the heart is.

All trust not based on the Word of God is vain.

UNBELIEF

Unbelief is nothing but the blasphemy of considering God a liar.

All unbelief is idolatry.

Alas, unbelief and distrust spoil everything and lead us into all kinds of misery, as we see in every walk of life.

Believers should be undismayed in all difficulties.......But the trouble is that this wretched, confounded unbelief cannot be checked. As it sees with its eyes, so it judges and acts. It will not venture to step out into the dark.

UNITY

Accursed be the love and the harmony for the preservation of which men endanger the Word of God.

WARFARE

A man, especially a Christian, must be a man of war.

WISDOM

Without Christ your wisdom is a twofold folly, your holiness and righteousness a twofold sin and blasphemy against God.

WORLD

There is no helping the world. No matter what attitude you take. It wants to belong to the devil.

The world is a thistle head; it points its prickles at you no matter in which direction you turn it.

WORRY

We should let God do the worrying. Your labour and effort are not contrary to faith; they are useful for the curbing of the flesh. But worrying is opposition to God.

We should not be full of any other care for ourselves than this: not to be full of care for ourselves and thus to rob God of His care for us.

WORSHIP

To worship God in spirit, is the service and homage of the heart, and implies fear of God and trust in Him.

Serving God and truly worshipping God consists in believing on Him whom the Father has sent, Jesus Christ.

WRATH

God shows His greatest wrath by being silent and saying nothing.

YOUTH

Nothing is more harmful to a young person than to let him have his way and not constantly to urge and drive him to decent behaviour and work.

A young person is like the juice of fruits. You cannot keep it; it must ferment.

If an injury that really hurts is to be done to the devil, it must be inflicted through the young people who are reared in the knowledge of God, spread God's Word, and teach it to others.

ZEAL

Such a one (one who loves God and His church) cannot do otherwise than display such zeal, no matter if someone may be offended by it. Even though pious hearts may think such action immoderate, nevertheless it is written that all Christians, but especially the Messiah, must have this zeal.

LIVING INSIGHTS AND ILLUSTRATIONS

The turbulent and eventful life of Martin Luther as the Hercules of the Reformation, is one which provides a vast storehouse of insights and illustrations. This collection of anecdotes gleaned from a wide variety of sources may be read with profit as a fragmented autobiography of his life. On the other hand some of them will also provide a wealth of material for preachers, teachers and other public speakers inspiring and giving encouragement to Christians facing the battles of life.

AT BIRTH, Martin Luther's name was Martin *Luder*. He later changed it to the more academically respectable *Luther*.

❖

As a boy Martin Luther was not mollycoddled. 'My father was a poor miner. My mother carried all her wood on her back. Such a hard life makes people hard. On account of a miserable nut my mother once beat me till the blood flowed. My father once flogged me so severely that I fled and had a grudge against him till he wooed me back. But they meant heartily well.' That experience made Luther a great teacher. 'One must punish so that the apple goes with the rod. Yea, verily; not the apple alone, not the rod alone, but apple and rod in proper proportion and at the right time and in the right place.'

❖

As a schoolboy, Luther preferred music to any other subject, and he became proficient at playing the lute. He gave away his lute when he entered the monastic cloister at age 21.

❖

On a hot day in July 1505, Martin Luther, then a young university student, was walking near the village of Sotternheim when a summer storm suddenly blew up. A bolt of lightning struck near him and knocked him to the ground. Filled with terror, Luther cried, "St Anne, help me! I will become a monk!" That was his "call" to Christian service.

❖

"I was a good monk," wrote Martin Luther, "and I kept the rule of my order so strictly that I may say that if ever a monk got to heaven by his monkery it was I. All my brothers in the monastery who knew me will bear me out. If I had kept on any longer, I should have killed myself with vigils, prayers, reading, and other work."

And yet, after all the works, he had no peace of heart or assurance of salvation.

❧

In 1510, Martin Luther visited Rome and anticipated receiving great spiritual help, but he was disappointed. He climbed Pilate's Staircase on his hands and knees, kissing each step and repeating the "Our Father" for each step. At the top of the staircase, he said, "Who knows whether it is so?" He came seeking certainties, but returned home only with doubts.

❧

Luther almost died at age 19. On his way home from school, a dagger pierced his leg, cutting an artery. Only because he was with a friend, who fetched a doctor, was his life saved. Lying at the edge of the road till the doctor came, he cried to the mother of Jesus, "O, Mary, help!" His Wittenberg friends later criticized him for appealing to Mary instead of Jesus.

❧

"If it had not been for Dr. Staupitz," said Martin Luther, "I should have sunk in hell."

It was Staupitz who pointed the terrified Luther to the merits of Jesus Christ. Sometimes Luther spent six hours in the confessional, examining his heart and naming his sins. "Man, God is not angry with you!" the weary confessor exclaimed. "You are angry with God."

Dr. Staupitz assigned Luther to earn his doctor's degree so that he might teach Bible at the university. Luther gave fifteen reasons why he could not undertake the assignment, the main one being that it would kill him. "Quite all right," Staupitz replied. "God has plenty of work for clever men to do in heaven."

Because of those studies in the Bible, Luther discovered justification by faith and spearheaded the Reformation.

❧

In the collection of Luther relics in the British Museum there are few objects more interesting than an original copy of the Ninety Five Theses, a printed broadsheet which Luther fixed on the church door at Wittenberg, on the memorable 17th October, 1517. Apart from the bearing upon Luther's history it recalls a custom common in the old days, especially in university towns, for public disputations, being held on any topic of the time, or upon general points of philosophy which the challenger of disputant chose to elect. Luther used this method to bring before the learned at Wittenberg the doctrine of Indulgences and other points raised in his conflict with Tetzel. The discussion could not fail to establish and to spread the doctrines maintained in opposition to Rome. The Wittenberg disputation was a notable event in the history of the Reformation.

❊

Martin Luther believed in the preaching of the Word of God. While in Wittenberg he preached three services each Sunday (services at five and nine in the morning, and a service in the afternoon). He preached in the church each day of the week, climaxing with a Saturday evening service. He always balanced his messages, using the gospels, Paul's epistles, the catechism, and the Old Testament. In 1528 Luther preached 195 sermons over the course of 145 days. There are about 2300 of Luther's sermons in his complete works.

❊

Since you have written to know about the device for my seal, I will send you my first thoughts of what I would have my seal express, as a sign-token of my theology.

First, there shall be a cross, black, in a heart which shall have its natural colour; that thereby I may remind myself that faith in the Crucified saves us. For if a man believes from the heart, he is justified.

But although it is a *black* cross, because it mortifies, and must also cause pain, yet it leaves the heart its own colour, destroying not its nature; that is, it does not kill, but preserves alive. For "the just shall live by faith," but by the faith of the Crucified.

Moreover, this heart shall be set in the midst of a white rose; to show that faith gives joy, consolation, and peace, and sets the heart as in a white festive rose. Yet not as the world gives peace and joy; therefore shall the rose be white and not red. For white is the colour of all angels and spirits.

This rose is set in a sky-blue field, because such joy in the spirit and in faith is a beginning of the heavenly joy to come, which is indeed infolded therein and embraced by hope, although not yet manifest.

And in this field shall be a golden ring, because this blessedness endures eternally in heaven, and has no end, and is precious above all joy and all riches, as gold is the highest and most precious of metals. Christ our dear Lord, be with your spirit until that life. Amen.

❈

His young son Martin had a little dog, with which he was playing. When his father saw it, he said, "This babe preaches the word of God in word and deed: for God says, 'Have dominion over the cattle;' – and the dog will suffer anything from the child."

❈

Luther once visited a dying student; the good doctor and professor asked the young man what he should take to God, in whose presence he was shortly to appear. The young man replied, "Everything that is good, dear father – everything that is good!" Luther, rather surprised, said, "But how can you bring Him everything that is good, seeing you are but a poor sinner?" The pious youth replied, "Dear father, I will take to my God in heaven a penitent, humble heart, sprinkled with the blood of Christ." "Truly," said Luther, "this is everything good. Then go, dear son; you will be a welcome guest to God."

❈

The enemies of Luther were no strangers to his character of disinterested generosity. At first they hoped he might be bought by money or honour. The pope asked one of his cardinals why they did not stop this man's mouth with silver or gold! To which his enemies replied, "This German beast has no respect for gold or honours."

It is said the devil once confronted Martin Luther with a tabulation of his sins. Luther asked, "Is that all?" "No!" said the devil, "There are many more." Martin Luther said, "Put them down." The devil sneeringly wrote them down, and Martin Luther said, "Is that all you can think of?" The devil said, "Yes. Now what?" "Now," said Martin Luther, "write beneath them all, 'The blood of Jesus Christ cleanseth from all sin.'"

At Wittenberg, Melanchthon had issued an order that all the students should rise when Luther entered to lecture. Although this was an ancient college custom, yet the humble Luther was not pleased with it, and said, "I wish Philip would give up this old fashion. These marks of honour always compel me to offer more prayers to keep me humble. If I dared I would almost retire without having read my lecture!" How different from the spirit of those who expect people to rise in mark of reverence for them, when they are only ministers of the people, and not having any personal qualities to command such external worship! The worthier a man the more humility he usually has!

A friend proposed to him that he should dedicate one of his writings to Jerome Ebner, a juris-consult of Nuremberg, who was then in great repute. "You have too high a notion of my labours," answered Luther, modestly; "but I myself have a very poor opinion of them. It was my wish, however, to comply with your desire. I looked, but among all my papers – which I never before thought so meanly of – I could find nothing but what seemed totally unworthy of being dedicated to so distinguished a person by so humble an individual as myself.

❖

It was against the wish and intention of Luther that a church should bear his name. "I pray you," he said, "leave my name alone, and do not call yourselves Lutherans, but Christians. Who is Luther? My doctrine is not mine! I have not been crucified for anyone. St. Paul (I Cor. 3) would not that anyone should call themselves of Paul, nor of Peter, but of Christ. How, then, does it befit me, who am but miserable dust and ashes, to give my name to the children of Christ? Cease, my dear friends, to cling to these party names and distinctions – away with them all! Let us call ourselves Christians, after Him from whom our doctrine comes

On June 13, 1525, Dr. Martin Luther and Katherine von Bora were married in a private ceremony at the Black Cloister, the 'converted monastery' where Luther lived. As the custom was, two weeks later there was a public ceremony at the church. A host of friends attended, and the couple received many choice gifts. Of course, the enemy immediately circulated slanderous stories about the couple, but few people believed them. One man said that their first child would be the Antichrist. Luther knew for the marriage of monks and nuns the punishment was death, and lawyer Jerome Schurf opposed the step, because it was against the laws of Church and State. The church historian Philip Schaff wrote: 'The domestic life of Luther has far more than a biographical interest. It is one of the factors of modern civilization. Without Luther's reformation, clerical celibacy, with all its risks and evil consequences, might still be the universal law in all Western churches. There would be no married clergymen and clerical families in which the duties and virtues of conjugal, parental, and filial relations could be practiced. Viewed simply as a husband – father and as one of the founders of the clerical family, Luther deserves to be esteemed and honoured as one of the greatest benefactors of mankind.'

At family devotions one morning, Luther read Genesis 22 and talked about Abraham's sacrifice of Isaac, "I would not believe it!" said Katherine. "God would not have treated his son like that!"
"But Katie," Luther quietly replied, "He did!"

※

During one very difficult period, Luther was carrying many burdens and fighting many battles. Usually jolly and smiling, he was instead depressed and worried. Katherine endured this for days. One day, she met him at the door wearing a black mourning dress.
"Who died?" the professor asked.
"God," said Katherine.
"You foolish thing!" said Luther. "Why this foolishness?"
"It is true," she persisted. "God must have died, or Doctor Luther would not be so sorrowful."
Her therapy worked, and Luther snapped out of his depression.

※

On Wednesday, September 20, 1542, his dearly loved daughter Magdalena died, not yet fourteen years of age. Praying at her bedside the sorrowing father said, "I love her much; but if it be Thy will, O God, to take her, I shall gladly know she is with Thee." When he asked her, "Magdalen, my little daughter, thou wouldst gladly remain here with they father, but thou wilt also readily go to thy other Father?" the dying child replied, "Yes, dear father; as God wills."
Beside her coffin, after she had departed, he said, "My beloved Lena, thou art well bestowed; thou shalt rise again, and shine like a star; nay, like the sun........Indeed, I rejoice in the spirit, but sorrow in the flesh; the flesh will not submit. Parting grieves us beyond all measure."
After the funeral he said: "My daughter is now provided for, body and soul. We Christians ought not to mourn; we know that it must be thus. We are most fully assured of eternal life, for God, who has promised it to us through His Son, cannot lie. God has now two

saints of my flesh. If I could bring my daughter to life again, and she could bring me a kingdom, I would not do it. Oh, she is well cared for! Blessed are the dead who die in the Lord! Whoever dies thus is assured of eternal life!" We seem again to hear the words of the bereaved father, sorrowing yet rejoicing, "Thou hast given, Thou hast taken away; blessed be Thy name!"

※

Writing to his wife about an old servant, Luther said, "We must dismiss old John with honour. We know that he has always served us faithfully, and we will not be niggardly to so worthy a servant. You need not remind me that we are not rich. I would gladly give him ten florins if I had them, but do not let it be less than five. He is not able to do much for himself. Pray help him any other way you can. Think how this money can be raised. There is a silver cup which might be pawned. Sure I am that God will not desert us. Adieu."

※

Luther's pleasures were simple. He greatly admired the paintings and carvings of Albert Durer, and his own books were almost the first to be ornamented by the engraver. He enjoyed a game of skittles and chess, sang with his lute, loved animals and birds, which he used to watch at their nest building. Of one he writes, "That little fellow has chosen his shelter, and is quietly rocking himself to sleep, without a care for tomorrow's lodging, calmly holding by his little twig, and leaving God to think for him."

※

Historian J.A.Froude has said in his short biography of Luther that 'Luther's mind was literally world wide; his eyes were for ever observant of what was round him. Being one of the most copious of talkers, he enabled his friends to preserve the most extraordinary monument of his acquirements and of his intellectual vigour. On reading *The Table Talk of Luther*, one ceases to wonder how this single man could change the face of Europe.'

❖

When Luther's puppy happened to be at the table, he looked for a morsel from his master, and watched with open mouth and motionless eyes. Luther said, "Oh, if I could only pray the way this dog watches the meat! All his thoughts are concentrated on the piece of meat. Otherwise he has no thought, wish or hope."

❖

Luther one day heard a nightingale singing very sweetly near a pond full of frogs, who by their croaking seemed as though they wanted to silence the melodious bird. Luther said, "Thus it is in the world. Jesus Christ is the nightingale, making the gospel to be heard; the heretics and false prophets the frogs, trying to prevent his being heard."

❖

Luther's wrote his best known hymn, "A Mighty Fortress" around 1527, and it is quite probable that it was written during his months of exile at the Wartburg Castle following his stand against the papacy at the Diet of Worms. Whatever its origin he based it on the opening words of Psalm 46. Thomas Carlyle has said that 'it has something in it like the sound of the Alpine avalanches or the first murmur of earthquakes.' The first line of this hymn is also inscribed on the tomb of Luther at Wittenberg.

❖

When in the Wartburg Luther dreaded being charged with having deserted the field of battle, and the thought became insupportable. "Rather would I be stretched on burning coals than stagnate here, half dead! Ah, nothing on earth do I more desire than to face my enemies." Next to the assurance of Divine protection, the recollection of Melanchthon consoled him in his grief. "If I perish," he wrote to his dear friend, "the Gospel will lose nothing. You will succeed me, as Elisha succeeded Elijah, with a double portion of my spirit." But calling to mind the timidity of Melanchthon, he added: "Minister of the Word! Keep the walls and towers of Jerusalem till our enemies shall strike you down. We stand alone; after me, they will strike you down. But the truth of God will yet prevail."

❖

Some of the crowd who accompanied him in the outset of his journey said, "There are many cardinals and prelates at Worms! You will be burnt alive, and your body be reduced to ashes, as they did with John Huss," "Though they should kindle a fire," he replied, "whose flames should reach from Worms to Wittenberg and rise up to heaven, I would go through it in the name of the Lord, and stand before them."

❖

One day, when he had entered into an inn, and the crowd was as usual pressing to see him, an officer made his way through, and thus addressed him, "Are you the man who has taken in hand to reform the papacy? How can you expect to succeed?" "Yes," said Luther, "I am the man. I place my dependence upon the Almighty God, whose word and commandment are before me." The officer, deeply affected, gazed on him with a look of kindly sympathy, and said, "Dear friend, there is much in what you say. I am a servant of the Emperor Charles, but your Master is greater than mine. He will help and protect you."

❖

It was during one of his visitation tours as Staupitz's vicar, that Luther first heard of the traffic in indulgences. When at the monastery of

Grinima, he was informed of the proceedings of Tetzel, the agent of Rome for this business. On being told of his impudent harangues to deceive the poor people and to extract money from them he quietly but firmly remarked, "I will make a hole in this drum, if God so will!"

Tetzel used to go about from place to place, attending the fairs and markets, where he addressed the people, to attract them from other stalls, and then his assistants went about with the "Buy! Buy! Buy!" of salesmen. "Come here, come here," shouted Tetzel; "by the will of the Holy Father and the Holy Curia at Rome, I visit this place," and then described his wares, which were not indulgences, in the milder ecclesiastical sense, but professedly pardons for all sorts of wickedness and crime. This vile system roused Luther's indignation, and he set himself vehemently to oppose it, with what results is well known. It was the first sound of conflict with Rome. The avowed object of Tetzel was to obtain funds for the building of St. Peter's, but he and his assistants lived well on the traffic.

Towards his old antagonist in the matter of indulgences, Luther acted in a truly noble and magnanimous spirit. As soon as he heard of his illness, which proved fatal, he wrote a kind letter to him full of expressions of sympathy and goodwill. And, alluding to Tetzel's position at that time, he observes, in another place, "I am sorry that Tetzel has got himself into such great trouble, in consequence of his character and conduct being exposed. If it had been possible, I would rather wish him to have repented and remained in honour, since my reputation can neither suffer by his honour nor increase by his disgrace." He thus showed that it was not the person but the evil principles and actions of Tetzel which he abhorred and condemned.

Luther arrived at Eisleben on January 28, 1546 and, although very ill, he took part in the conferences which ensued, up to February 17. He preached four times and revised certain ecclesiastical regulations. At supper that day he spoke a great deal about his approaching death. Someone asked him whether we should recognise one another in the next world. He replied he thought we should. On retiring he was accompanied by the master of the house and his sons. He went to the window and remained there for a considerable time in silent prayer. Two other friends joined him, and to those present he expressed a desire to sleep if only for a half hour for the good it would do him. Resting upon his bed he did fall asleep for an hour and a half. On awaking he said to those in the room, "What! Are you still there? Will you not go, dear friends, and rest yourselves?" They told him they would remain with him and then he began to pray, "Into thy hands I commend my spirit: Thou hast redeemed me, O Lord, God of truth."

After requesting of the others that prayer be made for the extension of the gospel, he fell asleep again for about an hour. Awaking, he expressed a feeling of great illness. Dr. Jonas sought to give some assurance of help, but he said he was getting worse and prayed again: "O my Father, Thou, the God of our Lord Jesus Christ, Thou, the source of all consolation, I thank Thee for having revealed unto me Thy well-beloved Son, in whom I believe, whom I have preached, and acknowledged, and made known; whom I have loved and celebrated. I commend my soul to Thee, O my Lord Jesus Christ! I am about to quit this terrestrial body, I am about to be removed from this life, but I know that I shall abide eternally with Thee."

He then repeated three times: "Into Thy hands I commend my spirit: Thou hast redeemed me, O Lord, God of truth." He closed his eyes and fell back on his pillow. Efforts were made to revive him, and this question was put to him: "Reverend father, do you die firm in the faith you have taught?" Luther opened his eyes, looked at Dr. Jonas, and replied, firmly and distinctly: "Yes." He then fell asleep; his breathing was more and more faint: at length he sighed deeply, and the great reformer was gone.

His body was conveyed in a leaden coffin to Wittenberg, where it was interred on February 22, 1546, with the greatest honours. He sleeps in the castle church, at the foot of the pulpit.

After Luther's death, the situation in Germany became critical, and war broke out. Katherine had to flee Wittenberg, and when she returned, she found her house and gardens ruined and all her cattle gone. Then the plague returned, and Katherine and the children again had to flee. During that trip, she was thrown out of a wagon into the icy waters of a ditch; and that was the beginning of the end for her. Her daughter Margaret nursed her mother tenderly, even as she had nursed others; but there was no recovery. She died on December 20 1552, at Torgau, where she is buried in St. Mary's Church.

On her monument are the words: 'There fell asleep in God here at Torgau the late blessed Dr. Martin Luther's widow Katherine von Bora.'

LUTHER'S PSALTER

One of Luther's most treasured personal possession was his Psalter. Someone asked him for his copy, promising him a new one in exchange for the old one which was ragged and well worn with usage. But Luther flatly refused saying, 'I am used to my old copy. A memory for places is very useful, and my mind is not so good as it used to be. I can turn to any verse in my own book.'

'Though a man of great physical vigour, Luther did the work of more than five men,' says a contemporary biographer of the reformer. It was his faith in God which was his main support. No one nourished his soul as a man of God by prayerful meditation more joyously and fervently than Luther did in the Scriptures, especially the Psalms which he affectionately called 'his little Bible.'

May we also, like the two disciples on the road to Emmaus, say, 'Did not our heart burn within us, while he talked with us by the way and opened to us the Scriptures.'

May Luther, whose own devotional life is a classic example of spirituality, speak to us across the centuries in this selection of his writings from the Psalms.

PREFACE TO THE PSALTER.

*Let the word of Christ dwell in you richly in all wisdom; teaching
and admonishing one another in psalms and hymns and spiritual
songs, singing with grace in your hearts to the Lord.
Colossians 3 vs. 16*

The Psalms not only present to us the common and simple speech
of the saints but their loftiest thoughts and words in which they talked
earnestly about the highest things with God Himself. This is the
greatest gift of the saints which their hymns pass on to us, so that we
know for certain how their hearts felt and their mouth spoke to God
and man.

For a human heart is like a ship on a wild sea, tossed about by all
the four winds of the world.

And such storms teach us to pray earnestly, to open our heart and
pour forth our inmost thoughts. For when a man is hemmed in by
fear and sorrow he speaks very differently about trouble than one
who is surrounded by joy, and he who is surrounded by joy speaks
very differently of happiness than one who is hemmed in by fear. It
does not come from the heart (people say) when a sad person laughs
or a glad person weeps, that is, the innermost heart is not revealed..

And do not most of the Psalms consist of such earnest prayer in
the midst of storms? And where are lovelier words of joy to be
found than in the Psalms of praise and thanksgiving? There you see
into the hearts of the saints, like looking into gay and beautiful
gardens, or even heaven. What sweet and fine and lovely flowers
bloom there from all kinds of lovely, happy thoughts about God and
His benefits! And again, where are sadder and more plaintive words
of sorrow to be found than in the penitential psalms? There we can
look into the hearts of the saints as into death, or even hell. How
dark and black it is there because of the sense of the wrath of God!
Thus, when they speak of fear and hope they use such vivid words
that no painter could make the pictures clear, and no Cicero or any
orator could so depict it.

THE ROAD TO SUCCESS
Blessed is the man that walketh not in the counsel of the ungodly,
not standeth in the way of sinners, not sitteth in the seat of the
scornful. But his delight is in the law of the Lord.
Psalm 1 vs. 1-2

Men are concerned with blessedness. There is no one who does not wish that it may be well with him, and does not dread the thought that it should be ill with him. Yet all have drifted from the knowledge of true blessedness. The philosophers have searched most diligently and erred most grievously, thinking blessedness to exist in virtue. They have only made themselves more unhappy than the rest by depriving themselves of the blessings both of this life and the life to come. The common people, on the other hand, have thought blessedness to consist of sensual pleasure. They have hoped, at least, to enjoy the good of this life.

The psalmist, drawing his doctrine from heaven and deploring all of man's efforts, gives this definition of blessedness: That man is blessed who loves the law of God. Blessed is the man who has found this pearl of great price. However, if he has not found this prize, he may search for the blessing of God without ever experiencing it.

❖

GOD'S POWER THROUGH WEAKNESS
Out of the mouth of babes and sucklings hast thou ordained
strength because of thine enemies, that thou mightest still the
enemy and the avenger.
Psalm 8 vs. 2

Why does Christ found such a kingdom? Why does He not send the heavenly Spirits and Princes, Gabriel, Michael and other angels, who could offer strong resistance to the enemy and break his power? For the enemy and avenger is a strong and powerful spirit. He is the god and prince of this world, having a strong and everlasting kingdom, and many other spirits under him, each of which is stronger than all the people on earth.

Answer: the Lord, our Master, does not will to use Gabriel or Michael for this purpose, but wills rather to ordain strength out of the mouth of babes and sucklings. For it pleases the Maker to despise this wicked, vain, and furious spirit and to mock him. Therefore, because He wills to ordain such strength He lowers Himself so much, is made man, and even makes Himself subject to all men; as it is written in Psalm 22: 'I am a worm and no man; a reproach of man and despised of people'. He goes about in poverty as He Himself says in Matthew 8. With such a weak body and mean appearance He attacks the enemy, allows Himself to be crucified and slain, and through His cross and death He overcomes the enemy and avenger.

Thus our Lord God lays aside the great and mighty power of the angels in heaven and takes the most unlearned, simple, and weak people on earth and sets them over against the wisdom and power of the devil and the world. Such are the works of God. For He is a God who quickens the dead, and calls that which is not, and it is. It is God's nature that he shows His divine Majesty and power through weakness. That is the way in which the Lord our God founds His Kingdom It is carried on in weakness, but out of that weakness strength shall come.

THE CHURCH IS HIS CROWN
Thou hast crowned him with glory and honour.
Psalm 8 vs. 5

He talks here about the royal adornment with which Christ, crowned as a king, will be glorious in this world and in the world to come. It is the custom to adorn kings when they are to appear in splendour. Christ, the king, will likewise be adorned not for Himself alone in His natural body, but also for us in His spiritual body, which is the Church. For He gathers His Church through the preaching of the Gospel, and adorneth her with His Holy Spirit. And this adornment is set over against His wretched appearance, of which Isaiah says (ch. 53) that the Son of Man has no form nor comeliness, and few to follow Him, at the time of His suffering.

His own people cry over Him: 'Crucify Him, crucify Him!' Even His own disciples desert Him and flee from Him. But after His resurrection He will be gloriously adorned, and a multitude of Christians will follow Him on earth. And that will be the beautiful adornment with which He will be crowned in this world.

※

THE PEARL OF THE PSALMS
The Lord is my shepherd; I shall not want.
Psalm 23 vs. 1

As little as a lamb can help the shepherd in trivial things but must depend upon him for all important needs, even less can a man direct himself in the concerns of salvation or find comfort, help and guidance. Rather must he depend upon God, his shepherd, for all things, for God is infinitely more willing and active in doing all he can for his sheep than the most loving shepherd.

Christ is the gentle and tender shepherd who goes into the wilderness to seek the lost and fainting lamb, and when he finds it, he lays it on his shoulders rejoicing. Who would not follow such a shepherd gladly! The gospel is the voice of the shepherd by which he calls his lambs. From this we learn that we receive grace, forgiveness of sins and eternal salvation. The voice of the gospel is precious to the sheep of Christ. They listen to it eagerly, understand it, and rule their lives by it. They do not heed a voice which sounds strange, but reject and flee from it.

※

FAITH VERSUS FEAR
The Lord is the strength of my life; of whom shall I be afraid?
Psalm 27 vs. 1

Yes, He gives peace even in the midst of temptation, yet He does it in such a way that all the time you are going uphill and downhill and uphill again. One moment it is night, the next day, and then it is soon night again. It is not always night and not always day, it changes from one to the other so that at one time it is night and another day, and soon, it is night again. That is how He rules His Christian Church, as we can see from all the stories of the Old and the New Testaments.

And this is called the power of the Lord, that He is not a counsellor and comforter who, when He has given us His Word turns away from us and does nothing more for us, but He helps in order to bring our sufferings to an end. If we are led into temptation, He gives us His faithful counsel, and fortifies us with His Word, so that we do not sink to the ground from weakness, but are able to remain on our feet. But when the hour is come and we have suffered enough, He comes with His power and we win through and gain the victory. We need both counsel, to comfort and uphold us in our sufferings, and power to win through to the end. All the Psalms give Christians strength in suffering – that is, they comfort us in our afflictions, so that our backs do not break, but we continue in hope and patience. Thus He leads all Christians. That is His way. Anyone who does not know that does not know what sort of a king Christ is.

※

GOD'S WONDERFUL WORKS
The earth is full of the goodness of the Lord.
Psalm 33 vs. 5

God's wonderful works which happen daily are lightly esteemed, not because they are of no import but because they happen so constantly and without interruption. Man is used to the miracle that God rules the world and upholds all creation, and because things daily run their appointed course, it seems insignificant, and no man thinks it worth his while to meditate upon it and to regard it as God's wonderful work, and yet it is a greater wonder than that Christ fed five thousand men with five loaves and made wine from water.

I often heard my father say, that he had heard from his parents, my grandparents, that there are on earth many more people eating than there could be sheaves gathered together from all the fields on earth in a year. Reckon up, and you will find that more loaves are eaten in a year than corn is cut and gathered. Where does all the bread come from? Must you not acknowledge that it is the wonderful work of God, who blesses and multiplies the corn in the fields, and in the barns, the flour in the bin and the bread on the table? But there are few who think of it and notice that those are the wonderful works of God.

❀

MATERIAL FOR GOD
Forsake me not, O Lord: O my God, be not far from me.
Psalm 38 vs. 21

I am alone, forsaken and despised by all, therefore do Thou receive me and do not forsake me. It is the nature of God that He creates out of nothing; therefore, God cannot make anything out of him who has not yet become nothing. Men, on the other hand, change one thing into another, which is a futile occupation.

Therefore God receives none but those who are forsaken, restores health to none but those who are sick, gives sight to none but the blind, and life to none but the dead. He does not give saintliness to any but sinners, nor wisdom to any but fools. In short: He has mercy on none but the wretched and gives grace to none but those who are in disgrace. Therefore no arrogant saint, or just or wise man can be material for God, neither can he do the work of God, but he remains confined within his own work and makes of himself a fictitious, ostensible, false, and deceitful saint, that is, a hypocrite.

THE FEARFUL HEART
My heart is sore pained within me; and the terrors of death are
fallen upon me
Psalm 55 vs. 4

All suffering laid upon the flesh can be endured. The heart can even despise all physical suffering and rejoice in it, but when the heart is tormented and broken, that is the greatest anguish and suffering of all. In bodily afflictions you suffer but half, for joy and happiness may still fill the soul and heart, but when the heart alone must bear the burden, it takes great and lofty spirits, and special grace and strength to endure it.

Why then does God let such suffering and affliction befall those whom He loves most?

First, because He wants to save His people from pride, so that the great saints who have received such special grace from Him should not venture to put their trust in themselves. Therefore it must be thus mingled and salted for them that they do not always possess the power of the Spirit, but that at times, their faith grows restless and their hearts faint, so that they perceive what they are and confess that they can achieve nothing unless the pure grace of God sustains them.

Again, God lets such affliction befall them as an example to others, to shake the self-confident souls, and to comfort those who are afraid.

In the third place comes the right and true cause why God acts thus, namely, in order to teach His saints where they should seek true comfort, and be content to find Christ and to abide with Him.

HE CARETH FOR YOU
Cast thy burden upon the Lord, and he shall sustain thee: he shall never suffer the righteous to be moved.
Psalm 55 vs.22

Whoever desires to be a Christian must learn to believe this, and to exercise this faith in all his affairs, in physical and in spiritual things, in doing and in suffering, in living and dying, and to cast aside all anxious thoughts and cares and throw them cheerfully off. Yet he must not throw them into a corner, as some have vainly tried to do, for they will not let themselves be stripped of their power so long as they are allowed to dwell in the heart, but you must cast both your heart and your care upon God's back, for He has a strong neck and shoulders, and can well carry them. And, moreover, He bids us cast them upon Him, and the more we cast on Him, the more He is pleased, for he promises that He will bear your burden for you, and everything that concerns you. 'Cast ye all your care upon him; for he careth for you.'

O, if a man could learn this casting off of his care, he would know by experience that it is true. But he who does not learn such casting off of his care, must remain a downcast, dejected, defeated, rejected, and hopelessly confused man.

❊

GOD'S OMNIPOTENCE
How terrible art thou in thy works!
Psalm 66 vs.3

A housewife should stand in sheer amazement if she really thought about this: today she has a set of fifteen eggs and she places them under a hen or goose. In four or six weeks time she has a basket full of little chickens or goslings. They eat and drink, and grow until they are full grown. Where do they come from? The eggs open when the time is come, and inside sit the chicks or goslings. They poke their little beaks through the shell and at last creep out. The mother hen or goose does nothing but sit on the eggs and keep them warm. It is God's almighty power that is at work within those eggs, making them turn into hens and geese.

Similarly with the fish in the water and with all the plants which grow from the earth. Where do they come from? Their first beginning is the spawn which floats in the water, and from this grow, by the Word and power of God, carp, trout, pike, and all kinds of fish, so that the water is swarming with fish. An oak, beech or fir tree grows out of the earth many feet thick and many yards high. What is its first beginning? Water and earth. The root draws its sap and moisture from the soil and forces it up with all its might so that the tree grows big and strong and tall.

What is the cause of this? God's omnipotence and the Word which the eternal, almighty Creator spoke: 'Let the waters bring forth abundantly the moving creature that hath life, and fowl that may fly in the open firmament of heaven. And the earth bring forth the living creature after his kind, cattle and creeping thing and beasts of his kind.' It is the Word and Omnipotence of God that brings it all about.

※

THE PROMISE OF HIS PRESENCE
Nevertheless I am continually with thee.
Psalm 73 vs. 23

If for the sake of God's Word hardship, sorrow, and persecution come to us, all which follow in the train of the holy cross, the following thoughts should, with God's help, comfort and console us, and should make us determine to be of good cheer, full of courage and confidence, and lead us to surrender the cause trustfully into God's gracious and fatherly will.

First, that our cause is in the hands of Him who says so clearly, 'No man shall pluck them from My hand'. It would not be wise to take our cause into our own hands, for we could and should lose it by our loose ways. Likewise all the comfortable words are true and do not lie, which say, 'God is our refuge and strength'. Has any man who puts his trust in God ever been put to shame? All who trust in God will be saved, and again: 'Thou Lord hast not forsaken them that seek Thee.' Thus it is really true that God gave His only begotten Son for our salvation. If God gave His own Son for us, how could He ever bring Himself to desert us in small things?

God is much stronger, mightier and more powerful than the devil. Thus says St. John: 'Greater is He that is in you than he that is in the world'. If we fall, Christ the Almighty King of this world, must suffer with us, and even if His cause should fall, we should wish rather to fall with Christ than to stand with the highest power on earth.

※

THROUGH THE CROSS

Blessed is the man whom thou chastenest, O Lord, and teachest him out of they law.
Psalm 94 v.12

It is highly necessary that we should suffer, not only that God may thereby prove His honour, might, and strength against the devil, but also because the great and precious treasure which we have, if it were given unto us without such suffering and affliction would make us snore in our security. And we can see – unfortunately it is a general thing – that many abuse the Holy Gospel, behaving as if they were freed from all obligations through the Gospel and that there is nothing more they need do, or give or suffer. This is a sin and a shame.

The only way our God can check such evil is through the cross. He must so discipline us that our faith increases and grows stronger, and we thus draw the Saviour all the deeper into our soul. For we can no more grow strong without suffering and temptation than we can without eating and drinking

Therefore since it is better that we should be given a cross than that we should be spared a cross, no man must falter and take fright at it. Have you not a good, strong promise wherein to take comfort? Nor can the Gospel advance except through us as we suffer willingly and bear our cross.

❖

A SUMMONS TO SING

O sing unto the Lord a new song; for he hath done marvellous things: his right hand, and his holy arm, hath gotten him the victory.
Psalm 98 vs.1

This is the new song about the new kingdom, new creatures, new men, born not of the law or of works but of God and the Spirit, who themselves are miracles and who work miracles in Jesus Christ our Lord.

And because the Holy Ghost commands us all to sing, it is certain that he also commands us to believe in the miracles which have been wrought and proclaimed for our sake. Therefore doubt and unbelief are here condemned, when they say, 'How can I be sure that God, by His authority or His arm (that is through His Son) has wrought such victories and miracles for my sake? Listen (says the Spirit): for you, for you, for you it was done. You, you, you should sing, and give thanks and be happy. That is My wish and will.'

FAITH MEANS WATCHING
I watch, and am as a sparrow alone upon the housetop.
Psalm 102 vs. 7

Let us not sleep like others, but let us watch and be sober, for temporal desires are to the eternal good as the images in a dream are to true pictures. Therefore sleep now is nothing but love and desire for creatures. But to be wakeful is to hold to the eternal good and to seek it and long for it.

But in this the Christian is alone and none is with him. All the others are asleep. And he says: 'On the roof': as if he said: the world is a house where they all lie shut in asleep, but I am outside the house, on the roof, not yet in heaven, and yet no longer on earth. The world is below me and heaven is above. Thus I hover in solitude between the life of the world and the life eternal.

FAITH AND THE FLESH
Who forgiveth all thine iniquities; who healeth all thy diseases.
Psalm 103 vs. 3

Understand it in this way, that Christians are divided into two parts – the inner being, which is faith, and the outer, which is the flesh. If you look on a Christian according to his faith, he is completely pure, for there is no impurity in the Word of God, and where it enters into a heart which clings to it, the Word inevitably makes the heart completely pure. All things are therefore perfect in faith, and that is why we are kings and priests and the people of God. But as our faith is in the flesh and we are still living on earth, we feel at times evil tendencies, such as impatience and fear of death, etc. Those are all still weaknesses of the old man, for faith has not yet completely penetrated and has not yet complete dominion over the flesh.

This you can see from the parable in the Gospel of St. Luke, chapter 10, which tells of the man who went from Jerusalem down towards Jericho and fell among robbers, who wounded him and left him half dead. Afterwards a Samaritan had compassion on him and bound up his wounds and looked after him, and paid the host of the inn to nurse him. There you may see that this man is no longer sick unto death, because his neighbour took care of him; rather, he is certain that he will live. And yet there is still something lacking, for he is not yet completely well. His life is saved, but his health is not yet perfect. He is still under the doctor, and needing attention.

In the same way, we have the Lord Christ and are sure of eternal life, but there is still something of the old Adam in our flesh.

THE PREVAILING CHRIST
The Lord said unto my Lord, sit thou at my right hand, until I make thine enemies thy footstool.
Psalm 110 vs. 1

Christ is seated on high awaiting the time when His enemies shall be made His footstool. That is His proper work. He does not sleep, but He watches us. He does not ask anyone to deputise for Him. He does it Himself. When people incline towards Him, He is present to help. If a man is tempted and he cries unto Christ, he will be helped. The Last Day is not yet come, and the flesh and sin and death still remain, but on the Last Day Christ will deliver up the Kingdom to His Father. Now He rules in our hearts. He comforts us, makes us clean, and intercedes for us. On the last Day all His Christians will rule in unity with Him, and they will be seated at the right hand of the Father. Then the last and proper enemy will be slain. Here on earth is still unstable faith, anxiety about food, and despair if ever God shows His displeasure. What is now our comfort? Christ, our Priest, who has atoned for us and looks upon us and sees our enemies and reminds the Father that He is our portion. When we feel this in our conscience, we have a sure access to the Father in every need. We fail to see this only because our eyes are not sufficiently penetrating to pierce the clouds and look into heaven, and be assured that Christ is our Advocate.

❋

THE DELIGHT OF THE DELIVERED
The sorrows of death compassed me, and the pains of hell gat hold
upon me: I found trouble and sorrow. Then called I upon the
name of the Lord: O Lord, I beseech thee, deliver my soul.
Psalm 116 vs. 3-4

When God has given us true faith, so that we walk in firm trust, having no doubt that He, through Christ, is gracious unto us, then we are in paradise. But before we do anything wrong, all that may be changed and God may allow our heart to faint, so that we think it is His will to snatch the Saviour from our heart. Then is Christ so veiled that we can have no comfort in Him, and the devil pours into our hearts the most terrible thoughts about Him, so that our conscience feels it has lost Him, and is cast down and disquieted as if there were nothing but God's wrath towards us, which we by our sins have well deserved.

Yea, even if we know of no open sins, yet the devil has the power to make sin out of what is no sin, and thus he frightens our heart and makes us anxious so that we are tormented by such questions as: Who knows whether God will have you and give Christ to you?

This is the direst and deepest temptation and suffering with which God now and again attacks and tests even His greatest saints, so that the heart feels that God has taken His grace away from us; that He no longer wills to be our God, and whithersoever man turns he sees nothing but wrath and terror. Yet is not every soul sorely tempted, nor does any man know what it is like unless he has experienced it. Only the strongest spirits could endure such blows.

❖

THE HEAVEN OF GRACE
For his merciful kindness is great toward us; and the truth of the lord endureth for ever. Praise ye the Lord.
Psalm 117 vs. 2

There is a kingdom of grace which is mightier in us and over us than all wrath, sin, and evil.

You must picture this kingdom in childlike fashion, as though through the Gospel God has built over us who believe in Him, a great new heaven, which is called the heaven of grace, and it is far greater and more beautiful than the heaven which you can see, and in addition it is certain, imperishable, and eternal.

Whoever lives underneath this heaven can neither sin nor abide in sin; for, it is a heaven of grace, everlasting and eternal. And if a man stumbles or sins, he does not fall out of this heaven, unless he does not wish to remain, but would rather go to hell with the devil, as the unbelievers do. And though sin makes itself felt or death shows its teeth, and the devil frightens you, far more grace is here to rule over our sin, and far more life is here to rule over death, and far more of God is here to rule over all the devils, so that sin, death, and the devil are nothing more in this kingdom than black clouds under the lovely sky, which hide it for a while, but are not able to cover and conceal it for ever, but must remain beneath it and suffer it to be above and to remain supreme. In the end they must all pass away.

All this cannot be wrought through works, but through faith alone.

❖

A SURE FOUNDATION
Except the Lord build the house, they labour in vain that build it.
Psalm 127 vs. 1

Let the Lord build your house and look after it. Do not interfere with His work. It falls to Him, not you, to look after it. Leave Him, who is Master of the house and runs it, to look after it. If much is needed in a house, do not worry, God is greater than a house. He who fills heaven and earth will surely be able to fill a house, all the more so because He has undertaken to do so and allows the Psalmist to praise Him for it.

But this does not mean that He forbids you to work. Work you should and must, but do not ascribe the fact that you have food to eat and that your house is furnished, to your work, but to God's grace and blessing alone. For where it is ascribed to a man's own work, covetousness and worry immediately raise their heads and the thought that much work will mean many possessions. Hence the strange contradiction occurs that some, who work extremely hard, have scarcely enough to eat, while others who work leisurely are blessed with all good things. This means that God will have the honour, for He alone makes things grow. For even if you were to till the earth for a hundred years, and do all the work in the world, you could not make it bring forth one blade of grass; but while you are asleep, and without your work, God will bring the blade out of the little grain, and He adds many grains according to His will.

TARRYING AND TRUSTING
I wait for the Lord, my soul doth wait, and in his word do I hope.
Psalm 130 v.5

There are some people who want to show God the goal and to determine the time and the manner and at the same time suggest how they wish to be helped; and if things do not turn out as they wish, they become faint-hearted, or, if they can, they seek help elsewhere. They do not wait upon God, rather God should wait for them, and be ready at once to help them in the way they have planned. But those who truly wait upon God ask for grace, and they leave it free to God's good pleasure how, where, and by what means He shall help them. They do not despair of help, yet they do not give it a name. They rather leave it to God to baptise and name it, however long it may be delayed. But whoever names the help does not receive it, for he does not await and suffer the counsel, will, and tarrying of God.

❈

THE HUMBLE REWARDED
Though the Lord be high, yet hath he respect unto the lowly.
Psalm 138 vs. 6

Behold the picture painted here of God, who makes known to us His true nature in that it shows Him as looking *downward. Upward* He cannot look, for there is nought above Him; *beside* Him he cannot look, for there is nought like unto Him. Therefore He can only look downward, beneath Himself. Wherefore, the simpler and the lowlier thou art, the brighter do God's eyes see thee.

In short, this verse teaches us rightly to understand God's nature in that it shows Him as looking down upon the lowly and despised, and he knows God aright who knows that He looks upon the lowly. From such knowledge springs forth love of God and faith in Him, so that we willingly abandon ourselves to Him and follow Him.

The truly humble never think of the result of their humility, but with a simple heart they look at what is lowly, live gladly with it, and are never aware of their own humility. But the hypocrites wonder why their honour lingers so long on the way; and their hidden and deceitful pride is not content with humble ways, but secretly they think higher and higher of themselves. Therefore a truly humble soul never knows of her own humility, for if she knew, she would be proud because she is aware of that noble virtue within her. But with her heart and mind and all her senses she cleaves to the lowly things, for she has them unceasingly before her eyes. They are the images which dwell with her, and while she keeps her eyes on them, she cannot keep them on herself or be aware of herself.

❖

THE BLESSINGS OF GOD
The eyes of all wait upon thee; and thou givest them their meat in due season.
Psalm 145 vs. 15

Mark now, that no animal works for its food, but each hath its peculiar task, and thereafter it seeks and finds its meal. The bird sings and flies, builds its nest and rears its young ones; that is its work, but its work does not feed it. Oxen plough, horses carry loads and got to battle, sheep produce wool; that is their work, but they do not live by it; but the earth brings forth grass and feeds them through the blessing of God.

In the same way man must work, but yet he must know that it is Another who feeds him, and not his work. It is the blessing of God, although his work appears to feed him, because God gives him nothing without his work: like the bird which neither sows nor reaps, and yet would die of hunger if it did not look for food. But that it finds food is not due to its own work but to the goodness of God. For who has provided the food that the bird may find it? For, where God does not provide no one can find, even though all the world should search and work themselves to death. This we can see with our eyes and grasp with our hands: and yet we do not believe. And again, where He is not the counsellor and preserver nothing is secure; though it may be fastened with a hundred thousand locks. It will be scattered to the winds, that no man will know where it has gone.

THE PRAYERS OF LUTHER

To know Martin Luther at his best, one must become acquainted with him as a man of prayer at the throne of grace. Few have prayed more fervently and powerfully than Luther, and few have so strongly exhorted others to do likewise by exhortation and example. He said, 'As a shoemaker makes shoes and a tailor coats, so should a Christian pray. Prayer is the Christian's business.'

Even in the most demanding days of the Reformation, prayer was Luther's business. One of his students gives us an insight of Luther at prayer.

No day passes that he does not give three hours to prayer, and those the fittest for study. Once I happened to hear him. Good God! how great a spirit, how great a faith, was in his very words! With such reverence did he ask, as if he felt that he was speaking with God; with such hope and faith, as with a father and a friend. 'I know,' he said, 'that Thou art our Father and our God. I am certain, therefore, that Thou art about to destroy the persecutors of thy children. If Thou doest not, then our danger is Thine too. This business is wholly Thine, we come to it under compulsion; Thou, therefore, defend….' In almost these words, I standing afar off, heard him praying with a clear voice. And my mind burned within me with a singular emotion when he spoke in so friendly a manner, so weightily, so reverently, to God.

That was Luther the man, with his Father and his Best Friend.

BEGIN THE DAY WITH GOD

In the name of the Father and of the Son and of the Holy Ghost. Amen. I thank Thee, my heavenly Father, through Jesus Christ, Thy dear Son, that Thou hast kept me this night from all harm and danger; and I pray Thee that Thou wouldst keep me this day also from sin and every evil that all my doings and life may please Thee. For into Thy hands I commend myself, my body and soul, and all things. Let Thy holy angel be with me that the wicked foe may have no power over me. Amen.

END THE DAY WITH GOD

In the name of the Father and of the Son and of the Holy Ghost. Amen. I thank Thee, my heavenly Father, through Jesus Christ, Thy dear Son, that Thou hast graciously kept me this day; and I pray Thee that Thou wouldst forgive me all my sins, where I have done wrong, and graciously keep me this night. For into Thy hands I commend myself, my body and soul, and all things. Let Thy holy angel be with me that the wicked foe may have no power over me. Amen.

FOR SPIRITUAL DESIRES

Oh, behold, my Lord Jesus Christ, my misery; needy and poor am I and yet so loathe to accept Thy remedy that I do not sigh for the riches of Thy grace. Set aflame in me, O Lord, the desire for Thy grace and faith in Thy promise that I may not offend Thee, my most gracious God, by my perverse unbelief and satiety.

CONFIDENCE IN THE FATHER'S LOVE

O Almighty God, in Thy boundless mercy Thou hast not only granted us permission but by Thine only beloved Son, our Lord Jesus Christ, hast bidden and taught us through His merit and mediation to look to Thee as Father and to call Thee Father, while Thou mightest in all justice be a stern Judge of us sinners, who have so often and so grievously offended Thy divine and most blessed will and thus have angered Thee. We beseech Thee, put into our hearts by this Thy mercy a comforting confidence in Thy fatherly love, and let us feel and taste the sweetness of childlike security that we may joyfully call Thee Father, may love Thee and call upon Thee in every time of need. Watch over us that we may remain Thy children and not be guilty of turning Thee, dearest Father, into a terrible Judge and ourselves from children into enemies.

It is also Thy will that we not only call Thee Father but that all of us together call Thee *our* Father and thus offer our prayers with one accord for all. Grant us, therefore, brotherly love and unity that all of us may know and regard one another as true brethren and sisters and pray to Thee, our one common Father, for all men and for every man, even as one child prays for the other to its father.

Let no one among us seek only his own interests, forgetting those of others before Thee. But all hatred, envy, and dissension laid aside, may we love one another as true and pious children of God and thus be able to say with one accord, not 'my Father' but '*our* Father.' And Thou art not an earthly father; but Thou art in heaven, a spiritual Father, who is not mortal and uncertain like an earthly and ordinary father, who cannot help himself. Thereby Thou showest us how immeasurably better a Father Thou art and teachest us to hold all earthly fatherhood, fatherland, friends, goods, flesh and blood as nothing compared with Thee. Therefore grant us, O Father, that we may also be Thy heavenly children. Teach us to think only of our souls and of our heavenly inheritance that out temporal fatherland and earthly lot may not deceive, hold, and hinder us or turn us altogether into children of this world, that we may say with a good and real reason, "Our *heavenly* Father," and may truly be Thy heavenly children.

FOR SPIRITUAL INSIGHT

Govern Thou us, O God, that we may see our weakness with spiritual eyes, may be led to recognise Thy Son, may be ruled by the Holy Spirit, and, purified and sanctified, may confess Thee. Amen.

FOR STEADFASTNESS

Merciful Father, everlasting God, who didst not spare Thine own Son but didst deliver Him up for us all that He might bear our sin on the cross, grant us that our hearts never fear or become discouraged in this faith, through the same, Thy son, Jesus Christ, our Lord. Amen.

FOR GRACE

O my dear Lord Jesus Christ, Thou dost know my poor soul and my great failings, which I confess and deplore before Thee alone with an open heart. Alas, I find that I do not have the kind of will and resolution I certainly ought to have and that I am daily falling as a failing, sinful human being. And Thou knowest that I desire to have such will and resolution, but my enemy leads me bound and captive. Redeem me, a poor sinner, according to Thy divine will, from every evil and temptation. Strengthen and increase in me the true Christian faith; grant me grace to love my neighbour with all my heart, honestly and as I do myself, as my brother. Grant me patience in persecution and in every adversity. Thou didst say to Saint Peter that he should forgive not only seven times and hast bidden us ask of Thee with confidence. So I come in reliance on this command and promise of Thine and confess and deplore before Thee all my trouble, for Thou art my true Pastor and the Bishop of my soul. Thy will be done and be blessed forever. Amen.

A PLEA FOR SPIRITUAL STRENGTH

Behold, Lord, here is an empty cask that needs to be filled. My Lord, fill it. I am weak in faith; strengthen me. I am cold in love; warm me and fill me with fire that my love may flow out over my neighbour. I do not have a firm, strong faith; I doubt at times and cannot fully trust God. O Lord, help me; increase my faith and trust for me. In Thee is locked the treasure of all my possessions. I am poor; Thou art rich and art come to have mercy upon the poor. I am a sinner; Thou art righteous. I pour forth a stream of sin; but in Thee are all fullness and righteousness.

CONFESSING CONFIDENCE IN THE CARE OF CHRIST

O Lord, I am Thy sin; Thou art my righteousness. Therefore I triumph and am secure; for my sin cannot overpower Thy righteousness, nor can Thy righteousness let me be or remain a sinner. Blessed Lord God of mine, my Mercy and Redeemer, in Thee only do I trust; never let me be ashamed. Amen

"THY WILL BE DONE"

O Lord God, heavenly Father, I am Thy creature; do Thou with me whatever Thou dost please; it is all the same to me, for I know that I am surely Thine. And if it please Thee that I die this hour or suffer some great misfortune, I would still be very glad to suffer it. Never do I want to consider my life, honour, goods, and whatever I have as higher and greater than Thy will. Thy will shall please me at all times throughout my life.

PRAYER FOR THE SPIRIT OF THANKSGIVING

Lord God, heavenly Father, from whom we so superabundantly receive all manner of good without ceasing and by whom we are daily so graciously protected from all evil, let us through Thy Spirit wholeheartedly recognise all this in true faith that we may thank and praise Thy gentle goodness and mercy both here and hereafter in eternity, through Jesus Christ, Thy Son, our Lord. Amen

PREPARATION FOR THE LORD'S TABLE

Lord, what though it be true that I am not worthy that Thou shouldest come under my roof; yet I need and desire Thy help and grace that I, too, may become pious. So I come, relying on nothing but the welcome words that I have just heard, with which Thou hast invited me to Thy table and dost promise that I, an unworthy sinner, shall enjoy the forgiveness of all sins through Thy body and blood when I eat and drink it in this Sacrament. Amen. Dear Lord, Thy

Word is true. I do not doubt this, and so I eat and drink with Thee. Be it unto me according to Thy Word. Amen.

A PRAYER FOR EASTER

Almighty God, who through the death of Thy Son hast destroyed sin and death and through His resurrection hast restored innocence and eternal life that we, being delivered from the power of the devil, may live in Thy kingdom, grant that we may believe with our whole heart and, steadfast in this faith, ever praise and thank Thee, through the same Thy Son, Jesus Christ, our Lord. Amen

A PRAYER FOR MARRIAGE

O Lord God, who hast created man and woman and hast ordained them for the marriage bond, making them fruitful by Thy blessing, and hast typified therein the sacramental union of Thy dear Son, the Lord Jesus Christ, and the church, His bride, we beseech Thine infinite goodness and mercy that Thou wilt not permit this Thy creation, ordinance, and blessing to be disturbed or destroyed but wilt graciously preserve the same, through Jesus Christ, our Lord. Amen.

PRAYER OF A CHRISTIAN FATHER

Dear heavenly Father, since Thou hast placed upon me the name and the office of Thine honour and dost desire that I be called and honoured as father, grant me grace and bless me that I may rule and support my dear wife, children, and servants in a godly and Christian manner. Grant me wisdom and strength to rule and to raise them well, and give to them a good heart and will to follow Thy teaching and to be obedient. Amen.

AT THE ORDINATION OF A MINISTER

Lord God, heavenly, merciful Father, Thou hast commanded us to ask, to seek and to knock and hast promised to hear us if we call upon Thee in the name of Thy Son. On this Thy promise we rely, and we pray Thee to send this servant of Thy Word ... into Thy harvest, to stand by him, to bless his office and ministry, to open the ears of the believers for the blessed course of Thy Word that Thy name may be praised, Thy kingdom be increased, and Thy church grow. Amen.

AGAINST THE PERSECUTORS OF THE TRUTH

Awake, dear Lord God, hallow Thy name, which they are dishonouring; strengthen Thy kingdom, which they are destroying in us, and work Thy will, which they want to check in us. Nor, because of our sin, let them thus tread Thee underfoot who are not punishing our sin in us but want to extirpate Thy holy Word, Thy name, and Thy work in us, so that Thou be no God and have no people who preach, believe, and confess Thee.

AGAINST THOSE WHO DESECRATE GOD'S NAME LORD

God, dear Father, we beseech Thee to hallow Thy name both in us and in all the world. Destroy and exterminate the abominations, the idolatry, and the heresy of the Turk, the pope, and all false teachers and sectaries, who falsely bear Thy name and so shamefully misuse and so terribly blaspheme it. Boastfully they say that their teaching is Thy Word and the commandment of Thy church; and yet it is the devil's lie and fraud, whereby they miserably mislead so many poor souls in all the world and even kill them, persecuting and shedding innocent blood, thinking that thereby they are serving Thee. Dear Lord God, convert or restrain them.

Convert those who are to be converted, that with the right and pure doctrine and with a good and holy life they may hallow and praise Thy name with us, and we with them. But those who will not be converted restrain Thou, so that they must cease to abuse, disgrace, and dishonour Thy holy name and mislead poor people. Amen.

LUTHER PLEADS WITH GOD AT WORMS

Almighty, eternal God, what a contemptible thing this world is! Yet how it causes men to gape and stare at it! How small and slight is the trust of men in God! How frail and sensitive is the flesh of men, and the devil so powerful and active through his apostles and the wise of the world! How soon men become disheartened and hurry on, running the common course, the broad way to hell, where the godless belong! Their gaze is fixed only on what is splendid and powerful, great and mighty, and enjoys a reputation. If I, too, were to turn my eyes to such things, I would be undone; the verdict would already have been passed against me, and the bell that is to toll my doom would already have been cast. O God! O God! O Thou, my God, my God, help me against the reason and wisdom of all the world! Do this! Thou must do it, Thou alone! For this cause is not mine but Thine. For myself I have no business here with these great lords of the world. Indeed, I, too, desire to enjoy days of peace and quiet and to be undisturbed. But Thine, O Lord, is this cause. And it is righteous and of eternal importance. Stand by me, Thou faithful, eternal God! I rely on no man. Futile and vain is all, lame and halting all that is carnal and smacks of the flesh.

God, O God! Dost Thou not hear me, my God? Art Thou dead? Nay, Thou canst not die; Thou art merely hiding Thyself. Hast Thou chosen me for this task? I ask Thee. I am sure that Thou hast. Well, so let it be then; Thy will be done. For never in my life did I intend to oppose such great lords; never had I resolve to do this.

O God, stand by me in the name of Thy dear Son, Jesus Christ, who shall be my Protector and Defender, yea, my mighty Fortress, through the might and the strengthening of Thy Holy Spirit.

Lord, where tarries Thou? O Thou, my God, where art Thou? Come, oh, come! I am ready to lay down my life for this cause, meek as a lamb; for the cause is righteous, and it is Thine. I will not separate myself from Thee forever. Be that decision made in Thy name. The world must leave my conscience unconquered even though it were full of devils and though my body, the work and creation of Thy hands, should be utterly ruined. But Thy Word and Spirit are a good compensation to me. And, after all, only the body is concerned; the soul is Thine and belongs to Thee, and with Thee it will remain eternally. Amen. God help me. Amen.

FOR DELIVERANCE FROM ANTICHRIST

Come Lord Jesus Christ, and deliver us from the Antichrist; cast his throne into the abyss of hell, as he has deserved, so that sin and destruction may cease. Amen.

FOR THE END OF THIS WORLD OF LIES

O my Lord Christ, do come soon from heaven with fire and brimstone to put an end to such mockery and blasphemy! How most unbearably and intolerably men are outdoing themselves in wickedness!

THE REDEEMER'S RETURN

Grant, dear Lord God, that the blessed Day of Thy holy advent may come soon, so that we may be redeemed from this bad, wicked world, the devil's dominion, and be freed from the terrible plague which we must suffer from without and within, from wicked people and our own conscience. Do Thou dispatch this old maggot sack that we may finally get a different body, which is not full of sin, inclined to unchasteness and to everything evil, as the present one is, but one that is redeemed from all bodily and spiritual misery and made like unto Thy glorious body, dear Lord Jesus Christ, that we may at last come to our glorious redemption. Amen.

MARTIN LUTHER'S TEXT

For therein is the righeousness of God revealed from faith to faith: as it
is written, The just shall live by faith.   Romans 1 v. 17

BY FRANK W. BOREHAM

The moderator of the Church of Scotland once introduced
Frank W. Boreham as 'the man whose name is on all our lips,
whose books are on all our shelves, and whose illustrations are
in all our sermons.' Born in Tunbridge Wells, England he studied at
Spurgeon's Pastors College in London. The greater part of his ministry
took place in New Zealand, Tasmania and Australia. His famous series
on 'Texts that made History' lasted for some 125 Sunday evenings and
attracted large congregations.

This sermon on Martin Luther's Text is taken from 'A Bunch of
Everlastings' and was originally published by Epworth Press, 1920.

I. IT GOES without saying that the text that made Martin Luther made history with a vengeance. When, through its mystical but mighty ministry, Martin Luther entered into newness of life, the face of the world was changed. It was as though all the windows of Europe had been suddenly thrown open, and the sunshine came streaming in everywhere. The destinies of empires were turned that day into a new channel. Carlyle had a stirring and dramatic chapter in which he shows that every nation under heaven stood or fell according to the attitude that it assumed towards Martin Luther. 'I call this Luther a true Great Man,' he exclaims. 'He is great in intellect, great in courage, great in affection and integrity; one of our most loveable and gracious men. He is great, not as a hewn obelisk is great, but as an Alpine mountain is great, so simple, honest, spontaneous; not setting himself up to be great, but there for quite another purpose than the purpose of being great!' 'A mighty man,' he says again; what were all emperors, popes and potentates in comparison? His light was to flame as a beacon over long centuries and epochs of the world; the whole world and its history was waiting for this man!' And elsewhere he declares that the moment in which Luther defied the wrath of the Diet of Worms was the greatest moment in the modern history of men. Here, then was *the man*; what was *the text* that made him?

II. Let us visit a couple of very interesting European libraries! And here, in the Convent Library at Erfurt, we are shown an exceedingly famous and beautiful picture. It represents Luther as a young monk of four and twenty, poring in the early morning over a copy of the Scriptures to which a bit of broken chain is hanging. The dawn is stealing through the open lattice, illuminating both the open Bible and the eager face of its reader. And on the page that the young monk so intently studies are to be seen the words: *'The just shall live by faith.'*
    'The just shall live by faith!'
    'The just shall live by faith!'
These, then, are the words that made the world all over again. And now, leaving the Convent Library at Erfurt, let us visit another library, the Library of Rudolstadt! For here, in a glass case, we shall

discover a manuscript that will fascinate us. It is a letter in the handwriting of Dr Paul Luther, the reformer's youngest son. 'In the year 1544,' we read, 'my late dearest father, in the presence of us all, narrated the whole story of his journey to Rome. He acknowledged with great joy that, in that city, through the Spirit of Jesus Christ, he had come to the knowledge of the truth of the everlasting gospel. It happened in this way. As he repeated his prayers on the Lateran staircase, the words of the Prophet Habakkuk came suddenly to his mind: *"The just shall live by faith."* Thereupon he ceased his prayers, returned to Wittenberg, and took this as the chief foundation of all his doctrine.'

> *'The just shall live by faith!'*
> *'The just shall live by faith!'*

The picture in the one library, and the manuscript in the other, have told us all that we desire to know.

III. *'The just shall live by faith!'*
    'The just shall live by faith!'

The words do not flash or glitter. Like the ocean they do not give any indication upon the surface of the profundities and mysteries that lie concealed beneath. And yet of what other text can it be said that, occurring in the Old Testament, it is thrice quoted in the New?

'The just shall live by faith!' cries the Prophet.

'The just shall live by faith!' says Paul, when he addresses a letter to the greatest of the European churches.

'The just shall live by faith!' he says again, in his letter to the greatest of the Asiatic churches.

'The just shall live by faith!' says the writer of the Epistle to the Hebrews, addressing himself to Jews.

It is as though it were the sum and substance of everything, to be proclaimed by prophets in the old dispensation, and echoed by apostles in the new; to be translated into all languages and transmitted to every section of the habitable earth. Indeed, Bishop Lightfoot as good as says that the words represent the concentration and epitome of all revealed religion. 'The whole law,' he says, 'was given to Moses in six hundred and thirteen precepts. David, in the fifteenth Psalm, brings them all within the compass of eleven. Isaiah reduces them to six; Micah to three; and Isaiah, in a later passage, to two. But Habakkuk condenses them all into one: *"The just shall live by faith!"'*

And this string of monosyllables that sums up everything and is sent to everybody – the old world's text: the new world's text: the prophet's text; the Jew's text: the European's text: the Asiatic's text: everybody's text – is, in a special and peculiar sense, Martin Luther's text. We made that discovery in the libraries of Erfurt and Rudolstadt; and we shall, as we proceed, find abundant evidence to confirm us in that conclusion.

IV. For, strangely enough, the text that echoed itself three times in the New Testament echoed itself three times also in the experience of Luther. It met him at Wittenberg, it met him at Bologna, and it finally mastered him at Rome.

It was at Wittenberg that the incident occurred which we have already seen transferred to the painter's canvas. In the retirement of his quiet cell, while the world is still wrapped in slumber, he pores over the epistle to the Romans. Paul's quotation from Habakkuk strangely captivates him.

'The just shall live by faith!'

'The just shall live by faith!'

'This precept,' says the historian, 'fascinates him. "For the just, then" he says to himself, "there is a life different from that of other men; and this life is the gift of faith!' This promise, to which he opens all his heart, as if God had placed it there specially for him, unveils to him the mystery of the Christian life. For years afterwards, in the midst of his numerous occupations, he fancies that he still hears the words repeating themselves to him over and over again.'

'The just shall live by faith!'

'The just shall live by faith!'

Years pass. Luther travels. In the course of his journey, he crosses the Alps, is entertained at a Benedictine Convent at Bologna, and is there overtaken by a serious sickness. His mind relapses into utmost darkness and dejection. To die thus, under a burning sky and in a foreign land! He shudders at the thought. 'The sense of his sinfulness troubles him; the prospect of judgment fills him with dread.

But at the very moment at which these terrors reach their highest pitch, the words that had already struck him at Wittenberg recur forcibly to his memory and enlighten his soul like a ray from heaven

'The just shall live by faith!"

"The just shall live by faith!"

Thus restored and comforted,' the record concludes, 'he soon regains his health and resumes his journey.'

The third of these experiences – the experience narrated in that fireside conversation of which the manuscript at Rudolstadt has told us – befalls him at Rome. 'Wishing to obtain an indulgence promised by the Pope to all who shall ascend Pilate's Staircase on their knees, the good Saxon monk is painfully creeping up those steps which, he is told, were miraculously transported from Jerusalem to Rome. Whilst he is performing this meritorious act, however, he thinks he hears a voice of thunder crying, as at Wittenberg and Bologna –

"The just shall live by faith!"

"The just shall live by faith!"

'These words, that twice before have struck him like the voice of an angel from heaven, resound unceasingly and powerfully within him. He rises in amazement from the steps up which he is dragging his body: he shudders at himself: he is ashamed at seeing to what a depth superstition plunged him. He flies far from the scene of his folly.'

Thus, thrice in the New Testament and thrice in the life of Luther, the text speaks with singular appropriateness and effect.

V. 'This powerful text,' remarks Merle D'Aubigne, 'has a mysterious influence on the life of Luther. It was a *creative sentence,* both for the reformer and for the Reformation. It was in these words that God then said, 'Let there be light!' and there was light!'

VI. It was the unveiling of the Face of God! Until this great transforming text flashed its light into the soul of Luther, his thought of God was a pagan thought. And the pagan thought is an unjust thought, an unworthy thought, a cruel thought. Look at this Indian devotee! From head to foot he bears the marks of the torture that he has inflicted upon his body in his frantic efforts to give pleasure to his god. His back is a tangle of scars. The flesh has been lacerated by the pitiless hooks by which he has swung himself on the terrible churuka. Iron spears have been repeatedly run through his tongue. His ears are torn to ribbons. What does it mean? It can only mean that he worships a fiend! His god loves to see him in anguish! His cries of pain are music in the ears of the deity whom he adores! This ceaseless orgy of torture is his futile endeavour to satisfy the idol's lust for blood. Luther made precisely the same mistake. To his sensitive mind, every thought of God was a thing of terror. 'When I was young,' he tells us, 'it happened that at Eisleben, on Corpus Christi day, I was walking with the procession, when, suddenly, the sight of the Holy Sacrament which was carried by Doctor Staupitz, so terrified me that a cold sweat covered my body and I believed myself dying of terror.' All through his convent days he proceeds upon the assumption that God gloats over his misery. His life is a long drawn out agony. He creeps like a shadow along the galleries of the cloister, the walls echoing with his dismal moanings. His body wastes to a skeleton; his strength ebbs away: on more than one occasion his brother monks find him prostrate on the convent floor and pick him up for dead. And all the time he thinks of God as One who can find delight in these continuous torments! The just shall live, he says to himself, by penance and by pain. The just shall live by fasting: the just shall live by fear.

VII. *'The just shall live by fear!'* Luther mutters to himself every day of his life. *'The just shall live by faith!'* says the text that breaks upon him like a light from heaven.

'By fear! By fear!'
'By faith! By faith!'

And what is faith? The theologians may find difficulty in defining it, yet every little child knows what it is. In all the days of my own ministry I have found only one definition that has satisfied me, and whenever I have had occasion to speak of faith, I have recited it. It is Bishop O'Brien's :-

'They who know what is meant by faith in a promise, known what is meant by faith in the Gospel; they who know what is meant by

faith in a remedy, know what is meant by faith in the blood of the Redeemer; they who know what is meant by faith in a physician, faith in an advocate, faith in a friend, know, too, what is meant by faith in the Lord Jesus Christ.'

With the coming of the text, Luther passes from the realm of *fear* into the realm of faith. It is like passing from the rigours of an arctic night into the sunshine of a summer day; it is like passing from a crowded city slum into the fields where the daffodils dance and the linnets sing; it is like passing into a new world; it is like *entering Paradise!*

VIII. Yes, it is like *entering Paradise!* The expression is his, not mine. 'Before those words broke upon my mind,' he says, 'I hated God and was angry with Him because, not content with frightening us sinners by the law and by the miseries of life, he still further increased our torture by the gospel. But when, by the Spirit of God, I understood these words –

"The just shall live by faith!"

"The just shall live by faith!"

- then I felt born again like a new man; I entered through the open doors into *the very Paradise of God!'*

'Henceforward,' he says again, 'I saw the beloved and Holy Scriptures with other eyes. The words that I had previously detested, I began from that hour to value and to love as the sweetest and most consoling words in the Bible. In very truth, this text was to me *the true gate of Paradise!'*

'An open door into the very Paradise of God!'

'This text was to me the true gate of Paradise!'

And they who enter into the City of God by that gate will go no more out for ever.

CLASSIC SERMONS BY
Martin Luther

With the truth of the Gospel in his heart, Martin Luther could do nothing else but proclaim it. Those who heard him preach and teach said that his words were 'half battles'. Philip Melancthon, his closest of friends said that the secret of Luther's effectiveness was that 'his words were born not on his lips but in his soul.'

He spoke from the heart to the heart and thus shook the world. His preaching was mostly the running commentary style – lively, relevant to life, direct, earnest and totally loyal to the Scriptures.

His attitude towards preaching is found in the famous words he spoke in Wittenberg Church in March 1522.

'I simply taught, preached, wrote God's Word: otherwise I did nothing...... The Word so greatly weakened the papacy that never a prince or emperor inflicted such damage upon it. I did nothing. The Word did it all. Had I desired to foment trouble, I could have brought great bloodshed upon Germany. Yea, I could have started such a little game at Worms, that the Emperor would not have been safe. But what would it have been? A mug's game. I left it to the Word.'

The four sermons which I have included will help you to understand why he was one of the most extraordinary preachers in the history of the church, and how his message is still relevant five centuries after his death.

JUSTIFICATION BY FAITH

❈

And he said unto his disciples, There was a certain rich man, which had a steward; and the same was accused unto him that he had wasted his goods. And he called him, and said unto him, How is it that I hear this of thee? give an account of thy stewardship; for thou mayest be no longer steward. Then the steward said within himself, What shall I do? for my lord taketh away from me the stewardship: I cannot dig: to beg I am ashamed. I am resolved what to do, that, when I am put out of the stewardship, they may receive me into their houses. So he called every one of his lord's debtors unto him, and said unto the first, How much owest thou unto my Lord? And he said, An hundred measures of oil. And he said unto him, Take thy bill, and sit down quickly, and write fifty. Then said he to another, And how much owest thou? And he said, An hundred measure of wheat. And he said unto him, Take thy bill, and write fourscore. And the lord commended the unjust steward, because he had done wisely: for the children of this world are in their generation wiser than the children of light. And I say unto you, Make to yourselves friends of the mammon of unrighteousness; that, when ye fail, they may receive you into everlasting habitations (Luke 16:1-9).

❈

Although in my little book *Christian Liberty and Good Works,* I have taught very extensively how faith alone without work justifies, and good works are done first after we believe, that it seems I should henceforth politely keep quiet, and give every mind and heart the opportunity to understand and explain all the Gospel lessons for themselves; yet I perceive that the Gospel abides and prospers only among the few; the people are constantly dispirited and terrified by the passages that treat of good works; so that I see plainly how necessary it is, either to write Postils on each Gospel lesson, or to appoint sensible ministers in all places who can orally explain and teach these things.

If this Gospel be considered without the Spirit, by mere reason, it truly favours the priests and monks, and could be made to serve covetousness and to establish one's own works. For when Christ says: "Make to yourselves friends by means of the mammon of unrighteousness; that, when it shall fail, they may receive you into everlasting habitations" (Luke 6:9); they force from it three points against our doctrine of faith, namely: first, against that we teach faith alone justifies and saves from sin; second, that all good works ought to be gratuitously done to our neighbours out of free love; third, that we should not put any value in the merits of saints or of others.

Against our first proposition they claim that the Lord says here: "Make to yourselves friends by means of the mammon of unrighteousness," just as though works should make us friends, who previously were enemies. Against the second, it is what He says: "That they may receive you into the everlasting habitations;" just as though we should do the work for our own sakes and benefit. And again the third they quote: "The friends may receive us into everlasting habitation;" just as though we should serve the saints and trust in them to get to heaven. For the sake of the weak we reply to these:

FAITH ALONE MAKES US GOOD, AND FRIENDS OF GOD

The foundation must be maintained without wavering, that faith without any works, without any merit, reconciles man to God and makes him good, as Paul says to the Romans: "But now the righteousness of God without the law is manifested, being witnessed by the law and the prophets; even the righteousness of God which is by the faith of Jesus Christ ... unto all them that believe" (Romans 3:21-22). Paul at another place says: "To Abraham, his faith was reckoned for righteousness;" so also with us. Again: "Therefore being justified by faith, we have peace with God through our Lord Jesus Christ" (Romans 5:1). Again: "For with the heart man believeth unto righteousness; and with the mouth confession is made unto salvation" (Romans 10:10). These, and many similar passages, we must firmly hold and trust in them immovably, so that to faith alone without any assistance of works, is attributed the forgiveness of sins and our justification.

Take for an illustration the parable of Christ: "Even so every good tree bringeth forth good fruit; but a corrupt tree bringeth forth evil fruit" (Matthew 7:17). Here you see that the fruit does not make the tree good, but without any fruit and before any fruit the tree must first be good, or made good, before it can bear good fruit. As He also says: "Either make the tree good, and its fruit good; or else make the tree corrupt, and its fruit corrupt: for the tree is known by its fruit. Ye generation of vipers, how can ye, being evil, speak good things?" (Matthew 12:33-34). Thus it is the naked truth, that a man must be good without good works, and before he does any good works. And it is clear how impossible it is that a man should become good by works, when he is not good before he does the good works. For Christ stands firm when He says: "How can ye, being evil, speak good things?" And hence follows: How can ye, being evil, do good things?

Therefore, the powerful conclusion follows. There must be something far greater and more precious than all good works, by which a man becomes pious and good, before he does good; just as he must first be in bodily health before he can labour and do hard work. This great and precious something is the noble Word of God, which offers us in the Gospel the grace of God in Christ. He who hears and believes this, thereby becomes good and righteous. Wherefore it is called the Word of Life, a Word of Grace, a Word of Forgiveness. But he who neither hears nor believes it, can in no way become good. For Peter says in Acts 15:9. "And he made no distinction between us and them, cleansing their hearts by faith." For as the Word is, so will the heart be, which believes and cleaves firmly to it. The Word is a living, righteous, truthful, pure and good Word, so also the heart which cleaves to it, must be living, just, truthful, pure and good.

What now shall we say of those passages which so strongly insist on good works, as when the Lord says in Luke 16:9: "Make to yourselves friends by means of the mammon of unrighteousness?"

And in Matthew 25:42: "For I was hungry, and ye did not give me to eat." And many other similar passages, which sound altogether as though we had become good by works. We answer thus:

There are some who hear and read the Gospel and what is said by faith, and immediately conclude that they have formed a correct notion of what faith is. They do not think that faith is anything else than something which is altogether in their own power to have or not to have, as any other natural human work. Hence, when in their hearts they begin to think and say: "Verily, the doctrine is right, and I believe it is true," then they immediately think faith is present. But as soon as they see and feel in themselves and others that no change has taken place, and that the works do not follow and they remain as before in their old ways, then they conclude that faith is not sufficient, that they must have something more and greater than faith.

Behold, how they then seize the opportunity, and cry and say, Oh, faith alone does not do it. Why? Oh, because there are so many who believe, and are no better than before, and have not changed their minds at all. Such people are those whom Jude in his Epistle calls dreamers who deceive themselves with their own dreams. For what are such thoughts of theirs which they call faith, but a dream, a dark shadow of faith, which they themselves have created in their own thoughts, by their own strength without the grace of God? They become worse than they were before. For it happens with them as the Lord says: "Neither do men put new wine into old wine-skins; else the sins burst, and the wine is spilled" (Matthew 9:17). That is, they hear God's Word and do not lay hold of it; therefore, they burst and become worse.

But true faith, of which we speak, cannot be manufactured by our own thoughts, for it is solely a work of God in us, without any assistance on our part. As Paul says to the Romans, it is God's gift and grace, obtained by one man, Christ. Therefore, faith is something very powerful, active, restless, effective, which at once renews a person and again regenerates him, and leads him altogether not a new manner and character of life, so that it is impossible not to do good without ceasing.

For just as natural as it is for the tree to produce fruit, so natural is it for faith to produce good works. And just as it is quite unnecessary to command the tree to bear fruit, so there is no command given to the believer, as Paul says, not is urging necessary for him to do good, for he does it of himself, freely and unconstrained; just as he of himself without command sleeps, eats, drinks, put on his clothes, hears, speaks, goes and comes.

Whoever has not this faith talks but vainly about faith and works, and does not himself know what he says or whether it tends. He has not received it. He juggles with lies and applies the Scriptures where they speak of faith and works to his own dreams and false thoughts, which is purely a human work, whereas the Scriptures attribute both faith and good works not to ourselves, but to God alone.

Is not this a perverted and blind people? They teach we cannot do a good deed of ourselves, and then in their presumption go to work and arrogate to themselves the highest of all the works of God, namely faith, to manufacture it themselves out of their own perverted thoughts. Wherefore I have said that we should despair of ourselves and pray to God for faith as the apostles did in Luke 17:5. When we have faith, we need nothing more; for it brings with it the Holy Spirit, who then teaches us not only all things, but also establishes us firmly in it and leads us through death and hell to heaven.

Now observe, we have given these answers, that the Scriptures have such passages concerning works, on account of such dreamers and self-invented faith; not that man should become good by works, but that man should thereby prove and see the difference between false and true faith. For wherever faith is right it does good. If it does no good, it is then certainly a dream and a false idea of faith. So, just as the fruit on the tree does not make the tree good, but nevertheless outwardly proves and testifies that the tree is good, as Christ says, "By their fruits ye shall know them." Thus we should also learn to know faith by its fruits.

From this you see, there is a great difference between being good, and to be known as good; or to become good and to prove and show that you are good. Faith makes good, but works prove the faith and goodness to be right. Thus the Scriptures speak plainly, which prevails among the common people, as when a father says unto his son, "Go and be merciful, good and friendly to this or to that poor person." He does not command him to be merciful, good and friendly, but because he is already good and merciful, he requires that he should also prove it outwardly towards the poor by his act, in order that the goodness which he has in himself may also be known to others and be helpful to them.

You should explain all passages of Scripture referring to works, that God thereby desires to let the goodness received in faith express and prove itself, and become a benefit to others, so that false faith may become known and rooted out of the heart. God gives no one His grace that it may remain inactive and accomplish nothing good, but in order that it may bear interest, and by being publicly known and proved externally, draw every one to God, as Christ says: "Let your light so shine before men, that they may see your good works, and glorify your Father which is in heaven" (Matthew 5:16). Otherwise it would be but a buried treasure and a hidden light. But what profit is there in either? Yea, goodness does not only thereby become known to others, but we ourselves also become certain that we are honest, as Peter says: "Wherefore, brethren, give the more diligence to make your calling and election sure" (2 Peter 1:10). When works do not follow, a man cannot know whether his faith is right; yea, he may be certain that his faith is a dream, and not right as it should be. Thus Abraham became certain of his faith, and that he feared God, when he offered up his son. As God by the angel said to Abraham: "Now I know, that is, it is manifest, that thy fearest God, seeing thou hast not withheld thy son, thine only son, from me" Genesis 22:12).

Then abide by the truth, that man is internally in spirit before God, justified by faith alone without works, but externally and publicly before men and himself, he is justified by works, that he is at heart an honest believer and pious. The one you may call a public or outward justification, the other an inner justification, yet in the sense that the public or external justification is only the fruit, the result and proof of the justification in the heart, that a man does not become just thereby before God, but must previously be just before Him. So you may call the fruit of the tree the public or outward good of the tree, which is only the result and proof of its inner and natural goodness.

This is what James means when he says in his Epistle: "Faith without works is dead" (2:26). That is, as the works do not follow, it is a sure sign that there is no faith there; but only an empty thought and dream, which they falsely call faith. Now we understand the words of Christ: "Make to yourselves friends by means of the mammon of unrighteousness". That is, prove your faith publicly by your outward gifts, by which you win friends, that the poor may be witnesses of your public work, that your faith is genuine. For mere external giving in itself can never make friends, unless it proceed from faith, as Christ rejects the alms of the Pharisees that they thereby make no friends because their heart is false. Thus no heart can ever be right without faith, so that even nature forces the confession that no work makes one good, but rather the heart must first be good and upright.

ALL WORKS MUST BE DONE FREELY AND GRATUITOUSLY WITHOUT SEEKING GAIN BY THEM

Christ means this when He says: "Freely ye have received, freely give" (Matthew 10:8). For just as Christ with all His works did not merit heaven for Himself, because it was His before; but He served us thereby, not regarding or seeking His own, but these two things, namely, our benefit and the glory of God his Father; so also should we never seek our own in our good works, either temporal or eternal, but glorify God by freely and gratuitously doing good to our neighbour. This Paul teaches the Philippians, "Let this mind be in you, which was also in Christ Jesus: who, being in the form of God thought it not robbery to be equal with God: but made himself of no reputation, and took upon him the form of servant, and was made in the likeness of men; and being found in fashion as a man, he humbled himself, and became obedient unto death, even the death of the cross" (Philippians 2:5-8). That is, for Himself He had enough, since in Him dwelt all the fullness of the Godhead bodily; and yet He served us and became our servant.

And this is the cause; for since faith justifies and destroys sin before God, so it gives life and salvation. And now it would be a lasting shame and disgrace, and injurious to faith, if any one of his life and works would desire to obtain what faith already possesses and bring with it. Just as Christ would have only disgraced Himself had He done good in order to become the Son of God and Lord over all things, which He already was before. So faith makes us God's children, as John 9:12 says: "But as many as received Him, to them gave He the right to become the children of God, even to them that believe on His name." But if they are children, then they are heirs, as Paul says, "How then can we do anything to obtain the inheritance, which we already have by faith?"

But what shall we say of passages that insist on a good life for the sake of an external reward as this one does: "Make to yourselves friends by means of the mammon of unrighteousness"? And in Matthew 19:17: "But if thou wouldst enter into life, keep the commandments." "Lay up for yourselves treasures in heaven" (6:20). We will say this; that those who do not know faith, only speak and think of reward, as of works. They think that the same rule obtains here as in human affairs, that they must earn the Kingdom of heaven by their works. These, too, are dreams and false views, of which Malachi speaks: "Oh, that there were one among you that would shut the doors, that ye might not kindle fire on mine altar in vain!" (Malachi 1:10). They are slaves and greedy self-enjoying hirelings and day labourers, who receive their reward here on earth, like the Pharisees with their praying and fasting, as Christ says.

However, in regard to the eternal reward it is thus: in as much as works naturally follow faith, as I said, it is not necessary to command them, for it is impossible for faith not to do them without being commanded, in order that we may learn to distinguish the false from the true faith. Hence the eternal reward also follows true faith, naturally, without any seeking, so that it is impossible that it should not, although it may never be desired or sought, yet it is appropriated and promised in order that true and false believers may be known, and that every one may understand that a good life follows naturally of itself.

As an illustration of this, take a rude comparison: behold, hell and death are also threatened to the sinner, and naturally follow sin without any seeking; for no one does wickedly because he wants to be damned, but would much rather escape it. Yet, the result is there, and it is not necessary to declare it, for it will come of itself. It is declared that man might know what follows a wicked life; so here, a wicked life has its own reward without seeking it. Hence, a good life will find its reward without any seeking it.

Now when Christ says, "make to yourselves friends," "lay up for yourselves treasures," and the like you see that He means: do good, and it will follow of itself without your seeking, that you will have friends, find treasures in heaven, and receive a reward. But your eyes must simply be directed to a good life, and care nothing about the reward, but be satisfied to know and be assured that it will follow, and let God see to that. For those who look for a reward become lazy and unwilling labourers, and love the reward more than the work, yea, they become enemies of work. In this way God's will also becomes hateful, who has commanded us to work, and hence God's command and will must finally become burdensome to such a heart.

IT IS NOT THE SAINTS, BUT GOD ONLY WHO RECEIVES US INTO THE EVERLASTING HABITATIONS, AND BESTOWS THE REWARD

This is so clear that it needs no proof. For how can the saints receive us into heaven, as every one himself must depend on God alone to receive him into heaven, and every saint scarcely has enough for himself? This the wise virgins prove, who did not wish to give of their oil to the foolish virgins, and Peter says: "The righteous is scarcely saved." And Christ declares: "No man hath ascended up to heaven, but He that descended out of heaven, even the Son of Man, who is in heaven" (John 3:13).

When then shall we reply to: "Make to yourselves friends out of the mammon of unrighteousness; that, when it shall fail, they may receive you into the everlasting habitations?" We say this: That this passage says nothing about the saints in heaven, but of the poor and needy on earth, who live among us. As though Christ would say: "Why do you build churches, make saints and serve my mother, Peter, Paul and other departed saints? They do not need this or any other service of yours, they are not your friends, but friends of those who lived in their days and to whom they did good; but do service to your friends, that is, the poor who live in your time and among you, your nearest neighbours who need your help, make them your friends with your mammon."

Again, we must not understand this reception into the everlasting habitations as being done by man; however, man will be an instrument and witness to our faith, exercised and shown in their behalf, on account of which God receives us into the everlasting habitations. For thus the Scriptures are accustomed to speak when they say, sin condemns, faith saves; that means, sin is the cause why God condemns, and faith is the cause why He saves. As man also is at all times accustomed to say, your wickedness will bring your misfortune, which means, your wickedness is the cause and source of your misfortune. Thus our friends receive us into heaven, when they are the cause, through our faith shown to them, of entering heaven. This is enough on these three points.

WHAT IS MAMMON?

In this connection we will explain three questions, that we may better understand the Gospel. What is mammon? Why is it unrighteous? And why does Christ command us to imitate the unjust steward, who worked for his own gain at his master's expense, which without doubt is unjust and a sin?

First, *mammon is a Hebrew word meaning riches or temporal goods,* namely, whatever any one owns over and above what his needs require, and with which he can benefit others without injuring himself. For *hamon* in Hebrew means multitude, or a great crowd or many, from which mahmon or mammon, that is, multitude of riches or goods, is derived.

Second, *it is called unrighteous,* not because obtained by injustice and usury, for with unrighteous possessions no good can be done, for it must be returned, as Isaiah 61:8 says: "I, the lord, love justice, I hate robbery with iniquity." And Solomon says: "Withhold not good from them to whom it is due, when it is in the power of they hand to do it" (Proverbs 3:27). But it is called unrighteous because it stands in the service of unrighteousness, as

Paul says to the Ephesian, that the days are evil, although God made them and they are good, but they are evil because wicked men misuse them, in which they do many sins, offend and endanger souls.

Therefore, riches are unrighteous, because the people misuse and abuse them. For we know that wherever riches are, the saying hold good: money rules the world, men creep for it, they lie for it, they act the hypocrite for it, and do all manner of wickedness against their neighbour to obtain it, to keep it, and increase it to possess the friendship of the rich.

But it is especially before God an unrighteous mammon because man does not serve his neighbour with it; for where my neighbour is in need and I do not help him when I have the means to do so, I unjustly keep what is his, as I am indebted to give to him according to the law of nature: "Whatever you would that men should do to you, do you even so to them" (Matthew 7:12). And again Christ says: "Give to him that asketh thee." And John in his first Epistle (1:17) says: "But whoso hath this world's goods, and seeth his brother have need, and shutteth up his bowels of compassion from him, now dwelleth the love of God in him?" And few see this unrighteousness in mammon because it is spiritual, and is found also in those possessions which are obtained by the fairest means, which deceive them that they may think they do no one any harm, because they do not coarse outward injustice, by robbing, stealing and usury.

In the third place *it has been a matter of very great concern to many to know who the unjust steward is whom Christ so highly recommends?* This, in short, is the simple answer: Christ does not commend unto us the steward on account of his unrighteousness, but on account of his wisdom and his shrewdness, that with all his unrighteousness, he so wisely helps himself. As though I would urge someone to watch, pray and study, and would say: "Look here, murderers and thieves wake at night to rob and steal, why then do you not wake to pray and study?" By this I do not praise murderers and thieves for their crimes, but for the wisdom and foresight, that they so wisely obtain the goods of unrighteousness. Again, as though I would say: An unchaste woman adorns herself with gold and seeks to tempt young men, why will you not also adorn yourself with faith to please Christ? By this I do not praise fornication, but the diligence employed.

In this way Paul compares Adam and Christ saying: "Adam was a figure of him that was to come." Although from Adam we have nothing but sin, and from Christ nothing but grace, yet these are greatly opposed to each other. But the comparison and type consisted only in the consequence of birth, not in virtue or vice. As to birth, Adam is the father of all sinners, so Christ is the father of all righteous. And as all sinners come from one Adam, so all the righteous come from one Christ. Thus the unjust steward is here typified to us *only* in his cunning and wisdom, who knows so well how to help himself, that we should also consider, in the right way, the welfare of our souls as he did, in the wrong way, that of his body and life. With this we will let it suffice, and pray God for grace.

PREACHING AND PERCEIVING THE WORD

❖

Then saith the woman of Samaria unto him, How is it that thou, being a Jew, askest drink of me, which am a woman of Samaria? For the Jews have no dealings with the Samaritans. Jesus answered and said unto her, If thou knewest the gift of God, and who it is that saith to thee, Give me to drink; thou wouldest have asked of him, and he would have given thee living water. John 4 vs. 9-10

❖

Look at how gently the Lord deals with this woman! He does not break off talking to her, but continues: "Dear daughter, it is true that I want you to give me a drink; for I am physically fatigued. However, I am not merely interested in a drink for my body; I am looking for something else. I am seeking you Samaritans that you may hear me. I would be happier to reverse the order and give you a drink. In fact, this is the reason for my presence here. I am asking for a drink to quench my physical thirst that I might have occasion to give you a drink. If you only realised what a gift is now to be found on earth, you would ask me for it, and I would give you a drink that would taste better than this water. It is of the utmost importance to recognise this gift and to know him who gives it. But neither the gift nor the giver is known." This is also our lament – and it will eternally remain so – that the great multitude despises this unspeakably precious treasure and fails to recognise the Giver of this gift. In fact, we too, who claim to be saints, pay it no heed and do not fully appreciate the value of this treasure offered to us through the gospel. My dear friends, how few there are among us who esteem this as genuine treasure, as an eternal gem, as everlasting life! There must be some, however, who will hazard life and limb for it. In Matthew 13 we read of a man who found a pearl in a field. He sold all his possessions in order to buy the pearl and field. Thus we find many who are willing to endure tortures because of it; they, too, will receive the drink. But the other crowd says flippantly: 'What do I care about it?' You will find a hundred thousand people who regard silver mined from the earth as a real treasure. They will not shrink from labouring night and day to acquire such a perishable treasure.

Would to God that we could gradually train our hearts to believe that the preacher's words are God's Word and that the man addressing us is a scholar and a king. As a matter of fact, it is not an angel or a hundred thousand angels but the Divine Majesty Himself that is preaching there. To be sure, I do not hear this with my ears or see it with my eyes; all I hear is the voice of the preacher, or of my brother or father, and I behold only a man before me. But I view the picture correctly if I add that the voice and words of father or pastor are not his own words and doctrine but those of our Lord and God. It is not a prince, a king, or an archangel whom I hear; it is he who declares that he is able to dispense the water of eternal life. If we could believe this, we would be content indeed. However, a fault which is manifest throughout the world and also in us is that we fail to recognise the gift and its giver. I, too, am not at all perfect in this respect; my faith is not as profound and strong as I should like to have it. Flesh and blood are an impediment. They merely behold the person or the pastor and brother and hear only the voice of the father. They cannot be induced to say: "When I hear the Word, I hear a peal of thunder, and I see the whole world filled with lightning." No, we cannot be brought to do that, and this is most deplorable. Flesh and blood are at fault. They refuse to regard the oral word and the ministry as a treasure costlier and better than heaven and earth. People generally think: "If I had an opportunity to hear God speak in person, I would run my feet bloody." If someone announced: "I know of a place in the world where God speaks and anyone can hear God there"; if I had gone there and seen and heard a poor pastor baptising and preaching, and if I had been assured: "This is the place; here God is speaking through the voice of the preacher who brings God's Word" – I would have said, "Well, I have been duped! I see only a pastor." We should like to have God speak to us in his majesty. But I advise you not to run hither and yon for this. I suppose we could learn how people would run if God addressed them in his majesty. This is what happened on Mount Sinai, where only the angels spoke and yet the mountain was wrapped in smoke and quaked. But you now have the Word of God in church, in books, in your home; and this is God's Word as surely as if God himself were speaking to you.

Christ says: "You do not know the gift." We recognise neither the Word nor the Person of Christ, but we take offence at his humble and weak humanity. When God wants to speak and deal with us, he does not avail himself of an angel but of parents, or the pastor, or of my neighbour. This puzzles and blinds me so that I fail to recognise God, who is conversing with me through the person of the pastor or father. This prompts the Lord Christ to say in the text: "If you knew the gift of God, and who it is that is saying to you, 'Give me a drink,' then I would not be obliged to run after you and beg for a drink. You would run after me and ask me for the living water. But since you do not know the gift and do not recognise him who is speaking with you, you despise me." Even if Christ did no more than greet us, it would be a treasure above all treasures; it would be honour and treasure enough. He has another treasure in store for us, however, which he reveals when he brings us forgiveness of sin and redemption from death, Devil, and hell, when he transforms us into heavenly people and illuminates our hearts. We can never express the value of this treasure adequately. We shall always fall short of recognising it fully and of esteeming it as we really and truly should.

It is just beginning to dawn on us that God's speaking to us is an inexpressibly precious gift and that we are honoured to be God's pupils and disciples. This is what is meant by knowing the nature of the gift and the person of the Doctor and Teacher. We and our hearers are just beginning to recognise that it is not a man we are listening to, but that it is God who is telling us things that contain an everlasting treasure. Therefore we are told again and again that we cannot speak about this subject enough; we must be like a stammering child. We cannot fathom what an incomprehensibly great treasure we possess in the divine Word. Nor do we really understand who this Person addressing us is or how excellent and exalted this Person is. If we did, it would impel us to boast of being followers, not of a king or of an emperor of God. People in the world are proud if they have a gracious lord, or if they are privileged to see a prince; it means much to them to stand in his presence and hear him speak. Now it is true that it is a treasure to have a gracious lord or to be a prince's counsellor. But look at the glory of the man who can say: "I am God's pupil; I hear him speak – not an angel, not a pastor or a prince, but God himself. I am his counsellor." For God says: "My message is an excellent gift, and by comparison the world's riches and glory are nothing but filth."

My dear friends, regard it as a real treasure that God speaks unto your physical ear. The only thing that detracts from this gift is our deficient knowledge of it. To be sure, I do hear the sermon; however, I am wont to ask: "Who is speaking?" The pastor? By no means. You do not hear the pastor. Of course, the voice is his, but the words he employs are really spoken by my God. Therefore I must hold the Word of God in high esteem that I may become an apt pupil of the Word. If we looked upon it as the Word of God, we would be glad to go to church, to listen to the sermon, and to pay attention to the precious Word. There we would hear Christ say: "Give me a drink!" But since we do not honour the Word of God or show any interest in our own salvation, we do not hear the Word. In fact, we do not enjoy listening to any preacher unless he is gifted with a good and clear voice. If you look more at the pastor than at God; if you do not see God's person but merely gape to see whether the pastor is learned and skilled, whether he has good diction and articulates distinctly – then you have already become half a Jacob. For a poor speaker may speak the Word of God just as well as he who is endowed with eloquence. A father speaks the Word of God as well as God does, and your neighbour speaks it as well as the angel Gabriel. There is no difference between the Word when uttered by a schoolboy and when uttered by the angel Gabriel; they vary only in rhetorical ability. It matters not that dishes are made of different material – some of silver, others of tin – or whether they are enamelled earthen dishes. The same food may be prepared in silver as in dishes of tin. Venison, properly seasoned and prepared, tastes just as good in a wooden dish as in one of silver. People, however, do no recognise the person of God but only stare at the person of man. This is like a tired and hungry man who would refuse to eat unless the food is served on a silver platter. Such is the attitude that motivates the choice of many preachers today. Many, on the other hand, are forced to quit their office, are driven out and expelled. That is done by those who do not know this gift, who assume that it is a mere man speaking to them, although, as a matter of fact, it is even more than an angel, namely, your dear God, who creates body and soul. This does not imply that we should despise and reject the gifts which God has distributed according to his own measure, more to the one and fewer to the other; for gifts are manifold. However, there is but one God who works through this multiplicity of gifts. One dare not despise the treasure because of the person.

Dear Lord, give us who are truly hungry the real bread and drink. This is what Christ wishes to do to us. But first we must learn to know the gift and the Teacher. Then we should be ready not only to give all to him but also to say: "Oh, dear Lord, give me some of the eternal water too! Without it I must die of eternal thirst and hunger."

THE DEATH OF ST. STEPHEN

And they stoned Stephen, calling upon God, and saying, Lord Jesus, receive my spirit. And he kneeled down, and cried with a loud voice, Lord, lay not this sin to their charge. And when he had said this, he fell asleep. Acts 7 vs. 59-60

The *epistle text* seems to be not at all difficult; it is plain. It presents in Stephen an example of the faith of Christ. Little comment is necessary. We shall examine it briefly. The first principle it teaches is, we cannot secure the favour of God by erecting churches and other institutions. Stephen makes this fact plain in his citation from Isaiah.

We must not, however, be led to conclude it is wrong to build and endow churches. But it is wrong to go to the extreme of forfeiting faith and love in the effort, presuming thereby to do good works meriting God's favour. It results in abuses precluding all moderation. Every nook and corner is filled with churches and cloisters, regardless of the object of church-building.

There is no other reason for building churches than to afford a place where Christians may assemble to pray, to hear the gospel, and to receive the sacraments, if indeed there is a reason. When churches cease to be used for these purposes, they should be pulled down, as other buildings are when no longer of use. As it is now, the desire of every individual in the world is to establish his own chapel or altar, even his own mass, with a view of securing salvation, of purchasing heaven.

It is not a miserable, deplorable error and delusion to teach innocent people to depend on their works to the great disparagement of their Christian faith? Better to destroy all the churches and cathedrals in the world, to burn them to ashes – it is less sinful even when done through malice – than to allow one soul to be misled and lost by such error. God has given no special command in regard to the building of churches, but he has issued his commands in reference to our souls – his real and peculiar churches. Paul says concerning them: "Ye are the temple of God ... If any man defile the temple of God, him shall God destroy" (I Cor. 3:16-17).

I continue to assert that for the sake of exterminating the error mentioned, it would be well to overthrow at once all the churches in the world and to utilise ordinary dwellings or the open air for preaching, praying, and baptising, and for all Christian requirements.

Especially is there justification for so doing because of the worthless reason the Papists assign for building churches. Christ preached for over three years, but only three days in the temple at Jerusalem. The remainder of the time, he spoke in the schools of the Jews, in the wilderness, on the mountains, in ships, at the feasts, and otherwise in private dwellings. John the Baptist never entered the temple; he preached by the Jordan River and in all places. The apostles preached in the marketplace and streets of Jerusalem on the day of Pentecost. Philip preached in a chariot to the eunuch. Paul preached to the people by the riverside, in the Philippian jail, and in various private dwellings. In fact, Christ commanded the apostles to preach in private houses. I presume the preachers mentioned were equally good with those of today.

You see now some reason why lightening strikes the costly Papist churches more frequently than it does other buildings. Apparently, the wrath of God especially rests upon them because there, greater sins are committed, more blasphemies uttered, and great destruction of souls and of churches wrought, than take place in brothels and in thieves' dens. The keeper of a public brothel is less a sinner than the preacher who does not deliver the true gospel, and the brothel is not so bad as the false preacher's church. Even were the proprietor of the brothel daily to prostitute virgins, godly wives, and nuns, awful and abominable as such action would be, he would not be any worse nor would he work more harm than those papistical preachers.

Does this astonish you? Remember, the false preacher's doctrine effects nothing but daily to lead astray and to violate souls newly born in baptism – young Christians, tender souls, the pure, consecrated virgin brides of Christ. Since the evil is wrought spiritually, not bodily, no one observes it; but God is beyond measure displeased. In his wrath he cries through the prophets in unmistakable terms, "Thou harlot who invitest every passerby!" So little can God tolerate false preaching, Jeremiah in his prayer makes this complaint: "They ravished the women in Zion, and the maids in the cities of Judah" (Lam. 5:11). Now, spiritual virginity, the Christian faith, is immeasurably superior to bodily purity; for it alone can obtain heaven.

Let us, therefore, beloved friends, be wise; wisdom is essential. Let us truly learn we are saved through faith in Christ and that alone. This fact has been made sufficiently manifest. Then let no one rely upon his own works. Let us in our lifetimes engage only in such works as shall profit our neighbours, being indifferent to testament and institution, and direct our efforts to bettering the full course of our neighbours' lives.

It is related of a pious woman, St. Elizabeth, that once upon entering a cloister and seeing on the wall a fine painting portraying the sufferings of our Lord, she exclaimed: "The cost of this painting should have been saved for the sustenance of the body; the sufferings of Christ are to be painted on your hearts." How forcibly this godly utterance is directed against the things generally regarded precious! Were St. Elizabeth so to speak today, the Papists assuredly would burn her for blaspheming against the suffering of Christ and for condemning good works. She would be denounced as a heretic, though her merits were to surpass the combined merits of ten saints.

Stephen not only rejects the conception of the Jews in regard to churches and their erection, but also denounces all their works, saying they have received the Law by the disposition of angels and have not kept it. So the Jews, in return, reprove Stephen as if he had spoken against the temple, and further, blasphemed the law of Moses and would teach strange works. True, Stephen could not rightly have charged them with failure to observe the Law so far as external works are considered. For they were circumcised, and observed the rules in regard to meats, apparel, festivals, and all Moses' commands. It was their consciousness of having observed the Law that led them to stone him.

But Stephen's words were prompted by the same spirit that moved Paul when he said that by the deeds of the Law, no one is justified in the sight of God, faith alone being the justifier. Where the Holy Spirit is not present to grant grace, man's heart cannot favour the Law of God; it would prefer the Law did not exist. Every individual is conscious of his own apathy and disinclination toward what is good, and of his readiness to do evil. As Moses says, "The imagination of man's heart is evil from his youth" (Gen. 8:21).

When Stephen declares the Jews always resist the Holy Spirit, he means to imply that through their works they become presumptuous, are not inclined to accept the Spirit's aid, and are unwilling their works be rejected as ineffectual. Ever working and working to satisfy the demands of the Law, but without fulfilling its least requirement, they remain hypocrites to the end. Unwilling to embrace the faith whereby they would be able to accomplish good works, and the grace of the Spirit that would create a love for the Law, they make impossible the free, spontaneous observance of it. But the voluntary observer of the Law, and no other, God accepts.

Stephen calls the Jews "stiffnecked, uncircumcised in heart and ears" because they refuse to listen and understand. They continually cry, "Good words, good works! Law, Law!" though not effecting the least thing themselves. Just so do our Papists. As their fore-fathers did, so do the descendants, the mass of this generation; they persecute the righteous and boast it is done for the sake of God and his Law. Now we have the substance of this lesson. But let us examine it a little further.

First, we see in Stephen's conduct love toward God and man. He manifests his love to God by earnestly and severely censuring the Jews, calling them betrayers, murderers, and transgressors of the whole Law, yes, stiffnecked and saying they resist the fulfilment of the Law and resist also the Holy Spirit himself. More than that, he calls them "uncircumcised in heart and ears." How could he have censured them any more severely? So completely does he strip them of every creditable thing, it would seem as if he were moved by impatience and wrath.

But whom today would the world tolerate were he to attempt such censure of the Papists? Stephen's love for God constrained him to his act. No one who possesses the same degree of love can be silent and calmly permit the rejection of God's commandments. He cannot dissemble. He must censure and rebuke every opposer of God. Such conduct he cannot permit even if he risks his life to rebuke it.

We must infer from Stephen's example that he who silently ignores the transgression of God's commands or any sin has no love for him. Then how is it with the hypocrites who applaud transgression, with calumniators and those who laugh and eagerly listen to and speak about the faults of others?

We have just had occasion to state that Stephen was a layman, an ordinary Christian, not a priest. But the Papists sing his praises as a Levite, who read the epistle or the Gospel lesson at the altar. The Papists, however, pervert the truth entirely. It is necessary for us, therefore, to know what Luke says. He tells how the Christians in the inception of the church at Jerusalem made all their possessions common property and the apostles distributed to each member of the congregation as he needed. But, as it happened, the widows of the Grecian Jews were not provided for as were the Hebrew widows; hence, arose complaint. The apostles, seeing how the duty of providing for these things would be so burdensome as to interfere in a measure with their duties of praying and preaching, assembled the multitude of the disciples and said: "It is not reason that we should leave the word of God, and serve tables. Wherefore, brethren, look ye out from among you seven men of honest report, full of the Holy Ghost and wisdom, whom we may appoint over this business. But we will give ourselves continually to prayer, and to the ministry of the word" (Acts 6:2-3).

So Stephen, in connection with six others, was chosen to distribute the goods. Thence comes the word "deacon", servant or minister. These men served the congregation, ministering to their temporal wants.

Plainly, then, Stephen was a steward, or an administrator and guardian of the temporal good of the Christians; his duty was to administer them to those in need. In course of time, his office was perverted into that of a priest who reads the epistles and gospel lessons. The only trace left of Stephen's office is the slight resemblance found in the duty of the nuns' provosts, and in that of the administrators of hospitals and of the guardians of the poor. The readers of the epistle and gospel selections should be, not the consecrated, the shorn, the bearers of dalmatics, and brushers of flies at the altar, but ordinary, godly, laymen who keep a record of the needy and have charge of the common fund for distribution as necessity requires. Such was the actual office of Stephen. He never dreamed of reading epistles and gospels, of bald pates, and dalmatics. Those are all human devices.

As to the question that may arise whether an ordinary layman may be allowed to preach: Thou Stephen was not appointed to preach – the apostles, as stated, reserved that office for themselves – but to perform the duties of a steward, yet when he went to the market-place and mingled among the people, he immediately created a stir by performing signs and wonders, as the epistle says, and he even censured the rulers. Had the Pope and his followers been present, they certainly would have inquired as to his credentials - his church passport and his ecclesiastical character. Had he been lacking a bald pate and a prayer book, undoubtedly he would have been committed to the flames as a heretic, since he was not a priest nor a clergyman. These titles, which the Scripture accord all Christians, the Papists have appropriated to themselves alone, terming all other men "the laity", and themselves "the church," as if the laity were not a part of the church. At the same time, these people of boasted refinement and nobility do not in a single instance fill the office or do the work of a priest, of a clergyman, or of the church. They but dupe the world with their human devices.

The precedent of Stephen holds good. His example gives all men authority to preach wherever they can find hearers, whether it be in a building or at the marketplace. He does not confine the preaching of God's Word to bald pates and long gowns. At the same time he does not interfere with the preaching of the apostles. He attends to the duties of his own office and is readily silent where it is the place of the apostles to preach.

In the second place, Stephen's conduct is a beautiful example of love for fellowmen in that he entertains no ill will toward even his murderers. However severely he rebukes them in his zeal for the honour of God, such is the kingly feeling he has for them that in the very agonies of death, having made provision for himself by commending his spirit to God, he has no further thought about himself but is all concern for them. Under the influence of that love, he yields up his spirit. Not undesignedly does Luke place Stephen's prayer for his murderers at the close of the narrative. Note also, when praying for himself and commending his spirit to God, he stood, but he knelt to pray for his murderers. Further, he cried with a loud voice as he prayed for them, which he did not do for himself.

How much more fervently he prayed for his enemies than for himself! How his heart must have burned, his eyes have overflowed, and his entire body been agitated and moved with compassion as he beheld the wretchedness of his enemies! It is St. Augustine's opinion that Paul was saved by this prayer. And it is not unreasonable to believe that God truly heard it and that from eternity he foresaw a great result from this dispensation. The person of Paul is evidence of God's answer to Stephen's prayer. It could not be denied, though all may not have been saved.

Stephen aptly chooses his words, saying, "Lay not this sin to their charge" (Acts 7:60), that is, make not their sin unremovable, like a pillar or a foundation. By these words Stephen makes confession, repents and renders satisfaction for sin, on behalf of his murderers. His words imply: "Beloved Lord, truly they commit a sin, a wrong. This cannot be denied." Just as it is customary in repentance and confession simply to deplore and confess the guilt. Stephen then prays, offering himself up, that abundant satisfaction may surely be made for sin.

Note how great an enemy at the same time how great a friend true love can be; how severe its censures and how sweet its aid. It is like a nut with a hard shell and a sweet kernel. Bitter to our old Adam nature, it is exceedingly sweet to the new man in us.

This epistle lesson, by the example given, inculcates the forcible doctrine of faith and love; and more, it affords comfort and encouragement. It not only teaches; it incites and impels. Death, the terror of the world, it styles a sleep; Luke says, "He fell asleep," that is, Stephen's death was quiet and painless; he departed as one goes to sleep, unknowing how, and unconsciously falls asleep.

The theory that the Christian's death is a sleep, a peaceful passing, has safe foundations in the declaration of the Spirit. The Spirit will not deceive us. Christ's grace and power make death peaceful. Its bitterness is far removed by Christ's death when we believe in him. He says, "If a man keep my saying, he shall never see death" (John 8:51). Why shall he not see it? Because the soul, embraced in his living word and filled with that life, cannot be sensible of death. The word lives and knows no death; so the soul which believes in that word and lives in it likewise does not taste death. This is why Christ's words are called words of life. They are the words of life; he who hangs upon them, who believes in them, must live.

Comfort and encouragement are further increased by Stephen's assertion, "I see the heavens opened, and the Son of man standing on the right hand of God" (Acts 7:56). Here we see how faithfully and lovingly Christ watches over us and how ready he is to aid us if we but believe in him and will cheerfully risk our lives for his sake. The vision was not given solely on Stephen's account; it was not recorded for his profit. It was for our consolation, to remove all doubt of our privilege to enjoy the same happy results, provided we conduct ourselves as Stephen did.

The fact that the heavens are open affords us the greatest comfort and removes all terror of death. What should not stand open and ready for us when the heavens, the supreme work of creation, are waiting wide for us and rejoicing at our approach? It may be your desire to see them visibly open to you. But were everyone to behold, where would faith be? That vision once given to man is enough for the comfort of all Christians, for the comfort and strengthening of their faith and for the removal of all death's terrors. For as we believe, so shall we experience, even though we see not physically.

Would not the angels, yes, all creatures, lend willing assistance when the Lord himself stands ready to help? Remarkably, Stephen saw not an angel, not God himself, but the man Christ, he who most delights humanity and who affords man the strongest comfort. Man, especially when in distress, welcomes the sight of another man in preference to that of angels or other creatures.

Our artful teachers who would measure the worlds of God by their own reason or the seas with a spoon, ask: "How could Stephen look into the heavens when our vision cannot discern a bird when it soars a little high? How could he see Christ distinctly enough to recognise him for a certainty? A man upon a high steeple appears to us a child, and we cannot recognise his person." They attempt to settle the question by declaring Stephen's vision must have been supernaturally quickened, permitting him to see clearly into infinite space. But suppose Stephen had been under a roof or within a vault? Away with such human nonsense! Paul when near Damascus certainly heard the voice of Christ from heaven, and his hearing was not quickened for the occasion. The apostles on Mount Tabor, John the Baptist, and again the people – these all heard the voice of the Father with their ordinary hearing. Is it not more difficult to hear a voice from a great distance above than to see an object in the same place? The range of our vision is immeasurably wider than the scope of our hearing.

When God desires to reveal himself, heaven and everything else requisite are near. It matters not whether Stephen were beneath a roof or in the open air; heaven was near to him. Abnormal vision was not necessary. God is everywhere; there is no need that he come down from heaven. A vision at close range of God actually in heaven is easily possible without the quickening or perverting of the senses.

It matters not whether or not we fully comprehend how such a vision is effected. It is not intended that the wonders of God be brought within our grasp; they are manifested to induce in us belief and confidence. Explain to me, ye of boasted wisdom, how the comparatively large apple or pear or cherry can be grown through the tiny stem; or even explain less mysterious things. But permit God to work; believe in his wonders, and do not presume to bring him within your comprehension.

Who can number the virtues illustrated in Stephen's example? There loom up all the fruits of the Spirit. We find love, faith, patience, benevolence, peace, meekness, wisdom, truth, simplicity, strength, consolation, philanthropy. We see there also hatred and censure for all forms of evil. We note a disposition not to value worldly advantage not to dread the terrors of death. Liberty, tranquillity, and all the noble virtues and graces are in evidence. There is no virtue but is illustrated in this example; no vice it does not rebuke. Well may the evangelist say Stephen was full of faith and power. Power here implies activity. Luke would say, "His faith was great; hence his many and mighty works." For when faith truly exists, its fruits must follow. The greater the faith, the more abundant its fruits.

True faith is a strong, active, and efficacious principle. Nothing is impossible to it. It rests not nor hesitates. Stephen, because of the superior activity of his faith, performed not merely ordinary works, but wrought wonders and signs publicly – great wonders and signs, as Luke says. This is written for a sign that the inactive individual lacks in faith, and has no right to boast of having it. Not undesignedly is the word "faith" placed before the word "power". The intention was to show that words are evidence of faith and that without faith, nothing good can be accomplished. Faith must be primary in every act. To this end may God assist us. Amen.

THE BIBLE IN MINIATURE

❈

For God so loved the world, that he gave his only begotten Son, that whosoever believeth in him should not perish, but have everlasting life. John 3 vs. 16

❈

Shortly before, Christ had said, "The Son of man must be lifted up, that whosoever believes in Him may have eternal life." Now He says, "God so loved the world that He gave His only Son, that whosoever believes in Him should not perish but have eternal life." What Christ said about the Son of man – that He must be lifted up - He now also says about the Son of God. He tells us that God's great love prompted Him to give His only Son. Earlier He said that Mary had given her Son, and now He says, "God the Father gave His Son to be crucified." God's Son and Mary's Son is only one Person. He appropriates both natures for the work of salvation and redemption from eternal death. John the evangelist always links the two natures, deity and humanity, together.

TWO NATURES

Someone may ask, "How is it possible for the Son of man to save and to give eternal life?" Or, "How can it be that God's Son should be delivered to be crucified?" It sounds plausible that the Son of man might be crucified, but that He should bestow eternal life does not seem reasonable. And it seems just as incongruous that God's Son should die and give His life for the life of the world. But we must bear in mind that when we speak of Christ, we are thinking of His two natures in one person and that what is ascribed to the two natures is really comprehended in one person. Thus, I can very properly say that the Son of man created heaven and earth, just as I say that the Son of God is the Creator of heaven and earth. We dare not follow those heretics, the Nestorians, the ancestors of the Turks, who allege that only Mary's Son, not God's Son, died for us. For here we find it clearly stated and written, "God gave His Son for the world." And this Son is assuredly not only Mary's Son, born of Mary, but also the Son of God. And when Christ was delivered to Pilate to be crucified, and when Pilate led Him from the judgment hall, he took hold of the hand not only of the man Jesus but also of the Son of God, whom he crucified. Therefore, Saint Paul said, "If they had understood, they would not have crucified the King of glory" (1 Cor. 2:8), whom all creatures usually adore. Thus, it was God's Son who was conceived by the Virgin Mary, who suffered and died, was buried, descended into hell, and rose again from the dead.

This is the way to interpret expressions of the apostles, bishops, and ancient teachers, "Oh, Thou Son of David!" or, "Thou Son of Mary, have mercy on me!" "Oh, dear Jesus, born of the Virgin Mary, be gracious to me!" The words are a prayer to God and are the equivalent of, "Oh, Jesus, Thou Son of God, have mercy on me!" In these words you also worship the Son of Mary, because the two natures are united in the one Christ.

ONE SON

Thus, the words of this text indicate that God gave His Son for us and that the Son of man died for us. There are not two Jesus, the one coming from the Father and the other born of Mary. No, there is only one Jesus. Therefore, the ancient fathers said that the attributes of both natures are ascribed and imputed to the whole person of Christ "in the concrete," creating a "communication of properties," a union in which the attributes of the one nature are imparted to the other. Each nature, of course, has its own peculiar character. For instance, it is peculiar to the human nature of Christ to be born of the Virgin Mary. The divine nature has different attributes. But since the person of Christ cannot be divided, there is a communion, which enables one to say, "The infant Christ, who lies in the cradle and is suckled by the Virgin Mary, created heaven and earth." Also, "The Son of God who is with the Father from eternity nurses at His mother's breasts, is crucified and dies." "For the communion of the natures also effects a communication of properties." The ancient fathers diligently taught this and wrote about it.

GOD INCARNATE

But now we have to make the practical application and learn why the person who is God and man came into the world. The Lord Christ teaches us this too, when He says that any believer in Him shall be delivered form eternal death and be assured of eternal life. It was not an angel, a principality, or any of the world's mighty who became incarnate and died for us – no, both the angelic and the human nature would have been too weak – but it was the divine nature that assumed humanity. It was Christ who adopted our flesh and blood that we might be saved through Him.

Now we see how gloriously the evangelist John speaks of Christ and of the sublime doctrine of our Christian faith: that Christ is both God and man. This is what John stresses in his Gospel. He says nothing about the necessity of good works for salvation, as the wicked pope does.

The Lord informed Nicodemus in an excellent sermon that no one will go to heaven or enter the kingdom of God unless he is born anew and believes in the serpent hanging on the cross, that is, believes in the Son of man, who was lifted up that all who believe in Him should not perish but have everlasting life. This is the new spiritual birth, the way to eternal life, namely, faith in the crucified Son of man. Now Christ stresses, and enlarges on, this theme in the fine sermon delivered to only one man, Nicodemus. It seems surprising that He should preach so beautifully to him. Yet His sermon is not in vain; it awakens in Nicodemus a love for Christ which does not only endure during the lifetime of Christ but lives on after His death (John 19:39). The end and aim of this sermon by Christ is the conversion of Nicodemus. The words, "For God so loved the world" do not need a lengthy commentary and exposition, for we preach on this text every year. Therefore our discussion will be brief.

After Christ has said, "As Moses lifted up the serpent in the wilderness, so must the Son of man be lifted up." He continues with the words, "For God so loved the world, that He gave His only Son, that whoever believes in Him should not perish but have eternal life." To astound Nicodemus, He repeats what He had said before. As though He wanted to say, "Dear Nicodemus, is it not wonderful that the Son of man is hanged on the cross and lifted up, and that the Son of man, born of the Virgin Mary, true man with body and soul, is also the Son of God? Is it not a miracle that the Son of man and the Son of God are both one Son? (For Christ relates the statement that whosoever believes in Him should not perish but have everlasting life to the Son of man and to the Son of God: this refers to both.) Thus, Nicodemus, I am preaching to you about very important matters which may well astonish you; for instance, about the necessity of the new birth. But still more amazing than this is the process of the new birth." It is, of course, out of the question for a man to re-enter his mother's womb to be born again. No, this is the procedure: God gave His only Son into death for us; that is how we are reborn. Does it not surprise you that for the sake of this rebirth God adopts such a wonderful plan and chooses His only Son – for He has no other – and lets Him become man, instead of selecting some angel or some patriarch? God does not confine Himself to giving us His Son in His incarnation, but He also delivers Him into death for us. He has Him lifted as Moses lifted up the serpent. Isn't that wonderful? Isn't that medicine effective enough? Who would ever have had the boldness to ask for such a cure for death and sin? But such strong help and powerful medicine will work this for you.

Now you do not understand all this, and you are wondering about this demand for a new birth and about this deliverance from sin. You know full well that we are sinners and are lodged in the jaws of death. Hence, it must sound odd and strange to you that we are to conquer sin and death and need not fear God's stern judgment and His wrath. Yes indeed, it is strange. But now behold! What is God's plan? The answer would never have occurred to you.

HE GAVE HIS SON

Because of His divine wisdom, counsel, and mercy God gives His only begotten Son, who is also the Son of man, as a remedy against sin, death, and your old nature and birth. The Son is "given" to us by dying for us and being buried for us. That, I take it, is another miracle and one far greater. If you are astonished and regard it as incredible that a man must be born anew, this greater wonder must amaze you still more. God loved a poor sinner so much that He gave him, not an angel or a prophet but His only Son. The way of His giving was that His Son became man, and the purpose of His giving was that He might be crucified. This you must learn; and after you have learned it and beheld these wonderful things, your heart will feel constrained to say, "This is truly miraculous! How is it possible?" But if you can accept and believe it, you will conclude, "After all, if God's Son is the cure and remedy for sin and death, why should I be surprised, since I know that God's Son is greater than sin, the devil, and my death?" Just believe it, and you will experience that He is greater. It is surely true that by my own strength I cannot banish death but must die even if I don a monk's cowl, join all the monastic orders and abide by their rules, go on pilgrimages, and perform all those good works on which they place all their reliance. None of this is the correct prescription or medicine. But if I can believe in and accept this remedy, that God gives us His Son – not an ordinary son like Abraham, Isaac, and David, of whom God has many, but His only begotten Son – it is certain that this son can effect a new birth in us and can, therefore, be a victor and conqueror of the devil. This is because God's Son is vastly greater than death, far stronger than sin and the devil. Through Him we have the grace of God rather than wrath, and whatever else we may need besides. If it puzzles you how a man is to be transferred from the devil's realm to the kingdom of God, God's gift of His Son must surprise you still more. And if you accept this in faith, you will no longer be puzzled about the other. If we have the Son of God, who faces death and opposes the devil on our behalf, on our side, let the devil range as he will. If the Son of God died for me, let death consume and devour me; for He will surely have to return and restore me, and I will stand my ground against him. Christ died; death devoured the Son of God. But in doing so death swallowed a thorn and had to get rid of it. It was impossible for death to hold Him. For this person is God; and since both God and man in one indivisible person entered into the belly of death and the devil, death ate a morsel that ripped [its] stomach open.

DEFEATING DEATH

It was the counsel of God the Father from eternity to destroy death, ruin the kingdom of the devil, and give the devil a little pill which he would gleefully devour, but which would create a great rumpus in his belly and in the world. Now the Lord wants to say, "Dear Nicodemus, it is miraculous, as you see, that God should spend such a great and precious treasure for our rebirth. For it is a miracle that I, the Son of man and the Son of God in one person, am sacrificed to death and enter the jaws of death and the devil? But I shall not remain there. Not only will I come forth again, but I will also rip open death's belly; for the poison is too potent, and death itself must die."

Christ wants to prevent us from thinking of Him as separate from the Father. Therefore He again directs our mind from Himself to the Father and says that the Father's love for us is just as strong and profound as His own, which is reflected in His sacrificial death. He wants to say, "Whoever beholds the Father's love also beholds Mine; for One love is identical. I love you with a love that redeems you from sin and death. And the Father's love, which gave you His only Son, is just as miraculous."

Furthermore, Christ tells us how he destroys death and how I am rescued from death. He will be death's venom. Death and [the] law, to be sure, will condemn Him. Therefore, He will have to die and be buried. But He will rise again from the dead. And where He is now, the devil will have to retreat. But how do I approach this Saviour and Redeemer? By means of cowls or monastic orders and rules? No! Just cling to the Son in faith. He conquered death and the devil, and he slit the devil's belly open. He will reign and rule again, even though He was crucified under Annas and Caiaphas. Therefore, attach yourself to Him, and you will tear through death and devil; for this text assures us, "Whoever believes in Him shall have eternal life." Accept the truth of this miracle of God's love for the world, and say "I believe in the Son of God and of Mary, who was lifted up and nailed to the cross." Then you will experience a new birth; for death and sin will no longer accuse, harm, and injure you. Whoever believes in the Son will have eternal life. Cling to His neck or to His garment; that is, believe that He became man and suffered for you; and say, "I am a Christian and will conquer." And you will find that death is vanquished. In Acts 2:24 Saint Peter says that death was not able to hold Christ, since deity and humanity were united in one person. In the same way we, too, shall not remain in death; we shall destroy death, but only if we remain steadfast in faith and cling to death's Destroyer.

In John 17:11 Christ prays, "That they may be one in Me, as I and the Father are one". If I cling to Christ in true faith and remain in Him, it is impossible for sin and death to accuse and condemn me; for Christ has conquered them. This, however, is accomplished, not by our strength but by faith in Him. In this way we, like pious lambs, remain resting in the arms of Christ, the faithful Shepherd.

OVERCOMING FEAR BY FAITH

Therefore, whoever is a Christian and takes hold of Christ by faith is not terrified by the devil; nor is he cowed by sin and death. Even though he feels his sins and is frightened and saddened by them, he nevertheless overcomes this feeling and is not subdued; for he will be quick to say, "I believe in the Son of God and of Mary. He is the devil's venom and death; but at the same time He is my salvation, my remedy, and my life."

We read an excellent story about a certain nun. (In every station of life God preserves some, keeps them in faith, and saves them.) This nun was very much troubled and assaulted by thoughts of the devil and of sin. Of course, all but those who serve their own belly feel God's wrath and judgment; this accounts for the fact that people will take refuge in the saints. Now, since this little nun was filled with terror at the thought of the wrath of God and wanted to be saved, she made it a habit to say whenever the devil troubled her, "Devil, let me alone. I am a Christian!" And the devil had to leave her. On the surface this seems to be a simple technique and easy to learn. But it is necessary that the words be inspired by faith, as those of this little nun were. For the devil did not particularly fear the words, "I am a Christian." No, it was her faith, the fact that she firmly relied on Christ and said, "I am baptised on Christ, and I entrust myself solely to Him; for He is my life, salvation, and wisdom." Wherever such words proceed from faith, they generate a completely fiery atmosphere, which burns and pains the devil so that he cannot tarry. But if a person speaks without warmth about matters pertaining to God and salvation, as the common man does, then the devil merely laughs. But if your words are aglow in your heart, you will put the devil to flight. For then Christ is present. As we read in Hosea 13:14, "He devours death and destroys it"; and here He declares, "Whoever believes in Me shall not perish but have everlasting life." If the believer is to have eternal life, it is implied that he is also free from sin and death. When the devil hears the name of Christ, he flees, because he cannot bear it. But if he does not feel the presence of Him who has destroyed him, he casts man into hell.

I am saying this for the sake of those who think that the mere recital of the words suffices, without any faith in the heart. Thus, many hear these words spoken and also resolve to use them on occasion. I want to tell you a story about this. An ungodly medical doctor in Italy was once asked to stand as godfather for an infant. During the rite of baptism he heard the beautiful words of institution, how the infant became an heir of salvation through Christ, and how the church implored God that Christ would accept this infant. After the baptism, when he pondered these words at home, he became very sad and depressed. As it happened, he had invited guests to dine with him that evening. When the guests noticed his melancholy mood, they asked him why he signed and why he seemed so troubled in his mind. Then he revealed his feelings and said, "I stood godfather today and heard some great and wonderful words. If I had the assurance that I was baptised in the same way, I would never again be terrified by the devil." One of the guests was an old man who had actually been godfather at this doctor's baptism. He spoke up, "Now my dear doctor, my dear doctor, you need not be in doubt on that score. For I was present in your baptism. I stood as godfather for you, and I can testify that you, too, were baptised this way." This made the doctor very happy. A little later he rose from the table and went to his room. There he noticed two large, long goat's horns projecting from a wall that had previously been bare. In an attempt to torment the doctor, the devil had assumed the guise of these horns. Now, when the doctor saw this, the thought flashed to him, "But I am baptised; I am a Christian. So why should I fear the devil?" Armed with that faith, he rushed to the wall and broke off one of the horns. Then he hurried back to his guests and joyfully related to them what had happened in the room. The guests all arose from the table and hurried into his room to see whether the one horn was still visible. Lo and behold, they found the two horns again protruding from the wall. One of the guests wanted to show off and imitate his host. He said, "Well, I am a Christian too!" And with these words he dashed towards the wall, intending to break off one of the horns. The devil broke his neck and killed him. The guest [had] tried to make light of the whole matter to deck himself with glory. In consequence, his head was torn off, whereas the doctor, who took recourse to faith in the hour of trial, suffered no harm.

This story is undoubtedly credible. My purpose in narrating it is to impress the fact that one must learn not only to recite the words of holy Scripture by rote but also to believe them with one's heart and to remain steadfast in times of peril and in the hour of death. For there are many who speak the words, "I am a Christian," with their mouth but do not believe this in their heart. When trouble besets you, you will find out whether you take these words seriously. In days of sorrow take hold of the Word of God and of Faith; pray, and say very fervently, "I am a Christian!" Then you will discover whether you really believe. When a person is not oppressed by sorrow, he has no occasion to perceive this. Callous people, who are not assailed by trouble or temptation, know nothing of this. The rebirth of which Christ speaks here is not acquired while dozing idly and comfortably behind the stove. If you are a Christian and really believe, join the nun in her words, "I am a Christian!" What is the result? You will find relief, and your mind will be at ease; and you will be able to thank God that the devil had to take to his heels. For he cannot withstand these words of fire.

BELIEVING IN GOD'S MIRACLE

Thus, it all depends on this great and grand miracle, that I believe that God gave His Son for us. If I do not doubt this, then I am able to say in the midst of my trials, I concede, devil, that I am a sinner burdened with the old Adam and subject to the wrath of God. But what do you, devil, say about this: God so loved the world that He gave His only Son that all who believe in Him might not perish but have eternal life? These words I believe!" And you must speak these words in sincere faith. For Christ has passed through death and sin, and death was powerless to hold Him. And now Christ says, "If you believe in Me, death shall not devour you either. Even if death should hold you for three days or so, as he detained Me for three days in the earth and Jonah for three days in the belly of the whale, he shall nonetheless spew you out again." You might have reason to be surprised about all this – not only that you must be born anew but also that God so loved the world that He gave us a potent plaster, remedy, and syrup against sin, death, the devil, and hell, so that whoever lays that on his heart will not perish.

On the other hand, consider the abominable error of those who directed us to other methods, telling people, for instance, that they should retire into the desert, enter cloisters, or go on pilgrimages – and all this so that we might not perish but have eternal life. I, too, entered the monastery that I might not perish but have eternal life. I wanted to follow my own counsel and help myself by means of the cowl. Truly, it is a vexing and troublesome business. In Turkey and in the papacy this doctrine is still rampant; the Jews teach the same thing. But it really comes from the mouth of the devil.

One might be tempted to ask, "Is it possible that so many can be mistaken about this?" The answer is that the Son of God is stronger than all the gates of hell (Matt. 16:18), also greater than all the monks and their cowls. Nicodemus, too, was curious to hear how he was to be reborn and saved from death. He asked how this was to happen. Jesus told him, "This is the way" the Son of man must be lifted up, and God's Son must be given into death, and man must believe in Him." Even if the world were to teem with monks' cowls and with monastic rules, even if the world were full of the ordinances of the pope, the Turks' Koran, or the Jews' laws, Christ would still be greater than all these. For He is still the Creator of heaven and earth and Lord over all creatures. His sacrifice for me was not Saint Francis or any other monk or the mother of Christ or Saint Peter or an angel or cowls and tonsures; it was a far move precious treasure. Salvation and deliverance from death call for a greater service than any human or any angel could render. Only God's only begotten Son can render it. The Son swallows up death.

RELYING ON CHRIST'S MERIT

Our adversaries also read this text, but they do not understand it. We also had these words in the papacy, but we failed to comprehend them. Instead, our thoughts were directed solely to our works. And yet some took hold of these words in faith and were saved, like the nun who said, "I am a Christian." I once saw a monk who took a cross into his hands and remarked while the other monks were boasting of their good works, "I know of no merit of my own but only of the merit of Him who died for me on the cross." And in reliance on that merit he also died. In the papacy it was customary to admonish a dying monk to be mindful of his own merits and works and of those of others. And in that faith they died. But just as the pious monk died a blessed death, relying solely on the merit of Jesus Christ, so many a wretched criminal on the gallows has been delivered from sin and saved through faith.

That is how Saint Bernard was saved. He was an exemplary monk; he observed the rules of his order scrupulously, and he fasted so assiduously that his breath stank and no one could abide his presence. But on the threshold of death he exclaimed, "Oh, I have lived damnably! But heavenly Father, Thou hast given me Thy Son, who has a twofold claim to heaven: first, from eternity, by reason of the fact that He is Thy Son; secondly, He earned heaven as the Son of man with His suffering, death, and resurrection. And thus He has also given and bestowed heaven on me." Thereby, Saint Bernard dropped out of the monastic role, forsook cowl and tonsure and rules, and turned to Christ; for he knew that Christ conquered death, not for Himself but for us men, that all who believe in the Son should not perish but have eternal life. And so Saint Bernard was saved.

These are golden words which must be preserved in Christendom; they alone make a person a Christian. You see how woefully those err who try to escape eternal damnation by means of their monkeries, cowls and tonsures. Moreover, such people even offer their supererogatory works for sale and transfer them to others. This, I regret to say, is how we lived in the papacy. You young people, be grateful to God for your better insight, and learn these words well. For death and the devil are in league with the pope and with the Turks' Koran to delude the people into relying on their foul works for salvation. But salvation demands more than our good works; for not even the holiness of the angels sufficed. God's own Son had to be given to conquer death. Now heaven and the victory over death are not Christ's alone; whoever believes in Him is not to perish but shall have eternal life. On the other hand, whoever refuses to believe is eternally beyond help and rescue, as Christ points out later when He says, "He who does not believe is condemned already" (John 3:18).

Christ said to Nicodemus, "God so loved the world." Furthermore, He assured him that God did not send His Son to condemn the world. From these words we learned that God's Son and the Son of man are one person. We learned that the Son of man was hanged and lifted up as the serpent in the wilderness had been lifted up. This applies properly only to His human nature, since God cannot suffer and be crucified. And yet Christ says here that the Son of God was given into death and was crucified. From this we learn about the communication of properties," the fact that the attributes of both natures inhere in the one person. Despite the fact that Creator and creature are two disparate beings, as different from each other as nothing is from something or from everything, or as different as heaven and earth, still it is true that here they are united.

ACCEPTING THE TESTIMONY OF SCRIPTURE

I am stressing this for a very good reason. Many heretics have arisen – and still more schismatic spirits will appear – who have assailed this article of faith and have been offended at the thought that God should suffer. The Godhead, they argued, is an eternal majesty, while humankind is only a temporal creature. They toyed with this article regarding the two natures in Christ most adroitly and alleged that Mary was not the mother of the Son of God, and that Christ, Mary's Son, is not the Son of God. They were offended by the two natures found in Christ. In place of the two natures they contrived to find two persons. According to holy Scripture, however, we declare that there are two natures in Christ but only one person and not two, and that this one person, God and man, suffered, that the Son of God and of Mary was crucified. A schismatic spirit may contradict this and say, "Ah, God cannot be crucified!" But tell them that this person, who is God and man was crucified. Since God manages to harmonise this, we, of course, must harmonise it too and declare that Mary is Christ's mother not only according to His humanity, but that she is also the mother of the Son of God and that her Son is both God and man. This is the language Saint Paul employs in Hebrews 6:6, when he speaks of the false Christians who "crucify the Son of God on their own account and hold Him up to contempt." And in 1 Corinthians 2:8 he says, "If they had understood, they would not have crucified the Lord of glory." Since it is the language of Saint Paul and of holy Scripture that the Son of God and the King of glory was crucified, we can accept it without hesitation. Anyone who believes the Bible will not mutter a sound against it. We can also reverse the picture and say, "This Infant, born of Mary and suckled by her or lying in her lap, created heaven and earth." If someone were to interpose, "Well, what, after all, could such a little child create?" I reply, "This is what holy Scripture says." For instance, in Luke 2:11 we hear the dear angels sing at Christmas time, "To you is born this day in the city of David a Saviour, who is Christ the Lord." That angelic song, in which Christ was called the Lord, was sung at a time when the Infant still clung to His mother's breast.

The fathers contended fervidly for this, maintaining against the heretics that there are two natures in Christ but not two persons, that there is only one Son. This is how Scripture speaks and how we, too, must speak. To be sure, Christ was crucified according to His humanity, and He created heaven and earth according to His divinity; but since this one person is God and man, it is proper to say that God's Son is the Creator of heaven and earth, and God's Son was also crucified. One dare not divide the person, leaving only the human nature; one must bear in mind that his person is also God. Thus Saint Hilary says, "When Christ suffered, the Logos was quiescent." If we fail to hold that the person who was crucified was both God and man, we are eternally damned and lost. We must have a Saviour who is more than a saint or an angel. If He were not superior to these, we would get no help from Him. But if He is God, then the treasure is so heavy that it not only outweighs and cancels sin and death but also gives eternal life. No mere human could acquire eternal life for us or overcome devil and death.

This is our Christian creed, and in conformity with it we confess, I believe in Jesus Christ, His only Son, our Lord, who was born of the Virgin Mary, suffered and died." Let heathen and heretics be ever so smart; hold firmly to this faith, and you will be saved. It follows, then, that whoever believes in the Son of man, who was born of Mary, who suffered and was buried, will not be lost but is a son of God in possession of eternal life. Devil, sin, and death will not be able to harm him, for he has eternal life.

WHOSOEVER BELIEVES ON HIM WILL NOT PERISH BUT HAVE EVERLASTING LIFE

The text has good reason for adding that God gave His *only* Son and that believers in Him will not perish but have eternal life. For God has many other sons. We, for instance, glory in the fact that God is our Father, as we pray in the Our Father. And Saint Paul declares that God "destined us in love to be His sons through Jesus Christ" (Eph. 1:5). But the evangelist identifies these sons when he says, "These are sons who believe in the Son." It is logical that the Son in whom we believe must be distinct and different and greater than we, the sons of God who believe in Him. Others are also sons of God, but they are not such sons as is He in whom we must believe. He is not a Son of God by reason of His believing in us; we, however, become sons of God through our believing in Him. Therefore, His divine sonship is vastly different from yours or mine.

The heretics garbled holy Scripture terribly. They claimed that Christ is called a Son of God by a metaphor, as we, too, are called sons of God. In Job 38:4, 7 the angels are also termed sons of God. We read, "Where were you when the sons of God [that is, all the angels] worshipped Me in heaven?" They claim that Christ was a son of God in that sense too. But scrutinise this text. Here we learn that He is the Son in whom we must believe. We holy people and the angels are not sons of God such as He is; for we all become sons of God through our faith in Him. The angels, too, were made sons of God through Him; for they were all created by the Son, as we read in Colossians 1:16. We human beings were also created by Him, but we lost and condemned sinners become sons of God through our faith in Him. Christ, however, is God and the Son of God; for there is a great difference between the one who believes and the in whom one believes. If someone deserves the honour that men believe in Him and through that faith become children of God and achieve the new birth, such a person must be very God. Again, if He created the angels and if the angels take first rank among the creatures, then Christ must be Lord of all creatures. Likewise, since He created us men, He cannot be a son of God in the sense in which we or John the Baptist are sons of God.

GOD'S UNIQUE SON

This is the real difference between the other sons of God and this Son of God. He is God Himself, whereas we are made sons of God through Him; He gives us eternal life and through Himself overcomes death. These are essential differences. This is how you must interpret holy Scripture, not only for your own sake but also to enable you to cope with the schismatic spirits, who twist and interpret Scripture according to their own ideas. You must realise that this Son is holy, safe from devil and death, and is not subject to damnation as we humans are. Nor does He require salvation for Himself; for He has always been, and still is, salvation and life personified. He is very God not only in His person but also in His office and His works. These bear witness to His divinity, as He says in John, "Even though you do not believe Me, believe Me for the sake of the works" (John 14:11). Therefore, it is a definition of His essence when this text says, "Whoever believes in Him has eternal life." It is He who bestows eternal life, kills death through Himself, and saves all who believe in Him. Such a work only God can do.

Your faith finds its vindication in the fact that Christ is very God in view not only of His essence and nature but also of His work. He is God in person, but He also performs the work of God: He saves those who believe in Him. Nowhere do we find it recorded that faith in any angel, whether Gabriel or Michael, or in John the Baptist or in the Virgin Mary, will make a person a child of God. Only of the Son is it said that He rescues from death and gives eternal life. Thus, Christ is established in the Godhead not only according to His person and majesty but also according to His work.

Therefore, it is fitting for us to write this text on every wall, and also in our hearts, with large, yes, with golden letters; for these are words of life and salvation. They teach us how to escape death and defend ourselves against all heretics, also against the pope and the Turk, all of whom read this text, but with drowsy eyes and deaf ears. For if they had heard, comprehended, and believed these words, they would not have fallen into such folly but would have said, "I am saved by Christ alone, who gave Himself into death for me." And if this is true, I am quick to add, "Well then, what am I doing in the cloister? Why did I run to Rome or to Saint James?" I did all this for the purpose of gaining salvation. And henceforth, I adjudge all religions and faiths false and heretical, whether of the Turk, of Mohammed, of the pope, or of the Jew, who also read and recite these words, but in the same indolent and indifferent manner in which the nuns read the Psalter without paying heed to its content. They too, speak these words, but they only repeat them by rote like a parrot. But you must reflect on these words and impress them on your heart. And after you have gained a good understanding of them, you are in a position to examine and judge faith and to stand your ground against the attacks of the schismatic spirits.

Christ says further, "Ponder this, dear Nicodemus: that God so loved the world that He gave His only Son, that [you] should be saved by Him." As if He were to say, "I Myself perform the work of redemption from sin and death." And this work performed by Him, He gives or transfers to the Father, so that the Father's work and the Son's work are one and the same. The evangelist John consistently distinguishes between the persons, but he identifies the work. For the Father is not the son of the Virgin Mary, nor was He crucified, but only the Son; and yet Father and Son remain true God, and the Son draws us to the Father through Himself.

GOD'S WRATH AND GOD'S LOVE

We heard Christ say, "That which is born of the flesh is flesh, and that which is born of the Spirit is spirit" (John 3:6); and, "No one has ascended into heaven but He who descended from heaven" (John 3:13). This is a hard and terrifying speech; it reflects nothing but the wrath of God. It condemns the whole world, deprives it of God, and leave it lost and condemned. Yes, God is a real tyrant. You have heard of God's anger and judgment; you have heard that we all were conceived and born in sin. But now hear of the love of God, that He looks with favour on you and loves you. If you wish to have a gracious God and Father and to know of His love for you, you must realise that you come to God by believing in the Son, whom the Father gave for you and who had Himself crucified for you. If this is your faith, it will be impossible for you not to feel the ineffable love of God manifested when He saved you from eternal doom and gave His Son that you might live. Hold firmly to this if you wish to be saved. For if you believe this, you ascend to heaven through Christ. Then you will not confront an angry judge but a dear Father, who is so kindly disposed towards you that He gave His Son for you; otherwise you would be lost. Now I can confidently say, "If God loved me so that He gave His only Son for my salvation, why should I fear His anger?"

In the papacy many sermons dealt with sin, death, and hell, and also with the wrath of God. But what did they say about deliverance from all this? They insisted that we render satisfaction for our sins with our good works and atone for them with monastic life, pilgrimages, and masses. But here we read, "Whoever does not believe in the Son has the wrath of God abiding over him." The pope, on the other hand, demands that I wear a cowl, be tonsured, and perform other tomfoolery to appease God's wrath. The Turk, the pope, and the Jews depict God as an angry God, but as one whose anger can be allayed and whose favour can be won if I humble myself, fast, sacrifice, perform good works, and expiate my sins with ascetic life. It is the devil himself who directs people to their good works and not to Christ, the Son of God. God forbids us to rely on ourselves and boast of our good works, no matter how good they may be; and He insists that we approach the Son, take hold of Him, cleave to Him, believe in Him, and say, "I believe in Jesus Christ, the only Son of God, who was born of the Virgin Mary, who suffered and died for me."

The papists sang this in their churches daily, and they also taught this creed to their children. However, no one understood it; otherwise no one would have said, "I want to escape hell with my monkery and my order." The Lord demands here that we refrain from all thoughts of finding God and attaining salvation by means of good works and seek refuge solely in Christ the Lord. For to seek God outside Christ leads to eternal damnation.

Much could still be said on this subject if time permitted. At all times there have been many schismatic spirits who ignored Christ and wanted to climb up into heaven and seek God with their clever thoughts and their good works. All the heresies that were rampant among the Jews can be traced back to the hermits or Levites, who erected altars in their gardens, in beautiful fields, in bright meadows, under a pretty linden tree, or on a hill,, whither they lured the people. Occasionally the devil would lend a hand with a miracle, and thus the people were miserably seduced. The prophets earnestly warned against this practice and condemned this self-devised zeal and worship of God. But when the clerics declared that this or that was to be done in these places because it was pleasing to God, the devil supported the suggestion. And the people flocked there in droves and established their own worship of God, just as though God were in agreement with them. He, however, had made it known through Moses where He wanted to be worshipped – not in any attractive spot, under a beautiful tree, in a gay meadow or field, or on a mountain, but at the place where the Ark of the Covenant rested. Thus, God was to be found only in the temple in Jerusalem. But the schismatic spirits retorted, "Why should God not also be found on this mountain or on the spot where Abraham, Isaac, and Jacob worshipped? God can hear us here as well as in Jerusalem." This meant climbing to God with one's own zeal.

TRYING TO CLIMB INTO HEAVEN

We did the same thing, We were not content with God's plan, "No one ascends into heaven but He who descends from heaven," and, "To escape damnation to attain eternal life, one must believe in the crucified Son." No, we replied, "You must assuredly perform good works, not only the good works prescribed in the Ten Commandments – oh, no, these do not suffice! You must also do the good works commanded by the pope, such as fasting, observing holidays, etc." And now these people mock us when we preach about faith. They say, "Faith? Nonsense! No, whoever joins this or that order is saved." This is the trouble. This means seeking God in our own arbitrary way and trying to climb into heaven on the self-invented ladder of our own ideas. We must be on our guard against the devil whose name is Enthusiasm. People who follow him disparage the oral Word and declare, "The Spirit must do it!" All they ever talk about is the Spirit. Of course, Nicodemus might have received the Spirit in this way too, but he gives ear to the Word of truth preached to him here by Christ, "No one ascends into heaven." The Word must still be preached and read orally, and the burden of our message must be, "I believe in the only Son of God, who died for me." We must seal our faith with the confession that we know of no other God than Him of whom we read here, "Whoever believes in the Son of man has everlasting life." No other thoughts or works will achieve this for me; the only way and the true way to God is to believe in the Son. Therefore, God has also commanded us to preach this diligently. That is why He established the ministry of oral preaching, instituted the sacraments, and commanded absolution. He wanted this message to remain alive among Christians that faith might be preserved in wakeful hearts, a faith which confesses, "I believe in the Son who was given into death for me."

The papist, to be sure, hear these words too; for they possess the Bible as we do. But they slumber and snore over the; they have eyes and do not see, ears and do not hear. They say, "Oh, if only I had done what Saint Augustine or Saint Francis commanded!" The laity call upon the Virgin Mary to intercede for them with her Son. During my twenty years in the cloisters I was obsessed with the one thought of observing the rules of my order. We were so drowned in the stupor of our own good works that we did not see and understand these words. But if you want to find God, then inscribe these words in your heart. Don't sleep, but be vigilant. Learn and ponder these words diligently, "God so loved the world that He gave His only Son, that whoever believes in Him should not perish but have eternal life." Let him who can write, write these words.

Furthermore, read them, discuss them, meditate and reflect on them in the morning and in the evening, whether awake or asleep! For the devil will sorely assail you faith in an effort to make you doubt that Christ is the Son of God and that your faith is pleasing to God. He will torture you with thoughts of predestination, with the wrath and the judgment of God. Then you must say, "I don't want to hear or know anything else about God than that He loves me. I don't want to know anything about a wrathful God, about His judgment and anger, about hell, about death, and about damnation. But if I do see God's wrath, I know that this drives me to the Son, where I find refuge; and if I come to the Son, I also have a merciful Father." For Saint John tells us in his epistle that the Father loved me before I ever loved Him or knew Him, that He remitted my sin and gave me salvation (1 John 4:10).

WORDS OF ETERNAL LIFE

Hearing these words and believing them makes a person a true Christian. But if one loses these words, all is lost, be you a Carthusian or whatever you will.

The words "not perish" are inexpressibly glorious. They mean to be rid of sin, to have a good conscience, and not to be under the law. Otherwise the law punishes sin; but now, even if someone feels sin and the wrath of God, sin will not give him a bad conscience, because his sin is forgiven. The law will not accuse him, sin will not bite or plague him, death will not devour him; for if he believes these words, he is safe and secure.

This is what we preach and believe. And let anyone who does not share this faith pray God that it may be imparted also to him. But see to it that you do not resist this faith or violate and blaspheme it, as the pope does when he says, "Of course, I know that Christ saves; but He does not save me." Well, the devil, too, knew that Christ saved Peter. Faith is not a paltry and pretty matter as the pope's contempt of it would make it appear; but it is a heartfelt confidence in God through Christ that Christ's suffering and death pertain to you and should belong to you. The pope and the devil have a faith too, but it is only a "historical faith." True faith does not doubt; it yields its whole heart to the conviction that the Son of God was given into death for us, that sin is remitted, that death is destroyed, and that these evils have been done away with – but, more than this, that eternal life, salvation, and glory, yes, God Himself have been restored to us, and that through the Son God has made us His children.

These are living words which Christ addresses to us, to you and to me, when He says that he who accepts the Son shall be saved and that death, devil, and hell shall be disposed of for him. These words comfort us when we are frightened and troubled or when we contend against the schismatic spirits. They extinguish the flaming darts of the devil (Eph. 6:16). They assure us that we retain the glory that god's Son is our gift and our treasure. This conviction cannot be imparted to us by any monastic order or rule, whether it be named for Saint Augustine or anyone else. No, you must say, "I believe in Christ, in whom Saint Augustine also believed." But if I were to say, "Oh, you dear Virgin Mary, you are holier than I. And you, Saint Francis, have many merits; transfer some of them to my credit!" it would all be vain. The same answer would be given to you that, according to Matthew 25:9, was given to the five foolish virgins when they wished to borrow from the wise virgins, who had their lamps full of oil: "Go to the dealers and buy for yourselves"; that is, go to your preachers and teachers, who misinformed you so.

Thus, we find rich, excellent, and salutary words in this text. They should be diligently heeded.